This exhibition catalogue

is made available to the

Portland Art Museum

through the generosity

of the

ROBERT LEHMAN FOUNDATION, INC.

Great Painters in Brescia

from the Renaissance to the 18th Century

From the Pinacoteca Tosio Martinengo

exhibition curated by
Penelope Hunter-Stiebel

catalog editors
Elena Lucchesi Ragni
Renata Stradiotti

linead'**ombra**libri

Front cover
Alessandro Bonvicino
called Moretto da Brescia, *Portrait
of a Gentleman with Letter*, ca. 1538
Pinacoteca Tosio Martinengo
Brescia

© 2006 Linea d'ombra Libri
Conegliano
© 2006 Comune di Brescia
All rights reserved
ISBN 88-89902-10-8
978-88-89902-10-3

Great Painters in Brescia
from the Renaissance
to the 18th Century

From the Pinacoteca Tosio Martinengo

Portland Art Museum, Oregon
April 29th - September 17th, 2006

Comune di Brescia

Settore Musei Civici
d'Arte e Storia

Linea d'**ombra**

BresciaMusei S.p.A.

Exhibition Curator
Penelope Hunter-Stiebel

Portland Art Museum

Former Executive Director
John E. Buchanan Jr.

Acting Executive Director
Judith L. Poe

Consulting Curator of European Art
Penelope Hunter-Stiebel

Registrar
Karen Christenson

Exhibitions Coordinator
Annalisa M. Borok

Exhibition Graphics Designer
Michael Smith

Head Preparator
Matthew Juniper

Catalog

Editors
Elena Lucchesi Ragni
Renata Stradiotti

Catalog essays and entries
Massimiliano Capella
Raffaella Colace
Angelo Dalerba
Francesco Frangi
Ida Gianfranceschi
Mina Gregori
Valerio Guazzoni
Elena Lucchesi Ragni
Marco Rossi
Rossana Sacchi
Renata Stradiotti

Bibliography
Anna Alberti

*Secretarial Office
and Organizational Coordinator*
Laura Rossi

Restorations
Gian Maria Casella
Garattini & Malzani
Marchetti & Fontanini
Romeo Seccamani

Photographs
Fotostudio Rapuzzi

General Coordination
Musei Civici d'Arte e Storia di Brescia
Renata Stradiotti
Director of the Museums
Elena Lucchesi Ragni
Curator of the Art and History Museums

*Technical-scientific, Graphic, Photographic,
Computer and Bibliographic Assistance*
Gerardo Brentegani
Luisa Cervati
Riccardo Manetti
Giampietro Marchesi
Claudio Perotti
Ugo Spini
Piera Tabaglio
Giuliana Ventura

with the assistance of all staff in the
Museum Section

Linea d'ombra

General Director
Marco Goldin

Executive Manager
Ida Bortoluzzi

Assistant Director
Davide Martinelli

International Loans
Zaira Bellet
Caterina Barbini
Paola De Troia

Iconographic Research
Fabiana Mei

Merchandising
Monica Braun

Graphic Design
Evelina Laviano

Editor
Silvia Zancanella

Bookings Manager
Federica Bertagnolli

Educational Activities Manager
Ornella Gabrieli

Insurance
Aon Artscope

Transport
Arterìa

Catalog

Graphic Layout
Evelina Laviano

Editor
Silvia Zancanella

Translations
David Graham

Review of Texts
Penelope Hunter-Stiebel

Printed by
Grafiche Antiga, Cornuda (Treviso)

Coordination
Piero De Luca
assisted by
Marianna Antiga

This extraordinary exhibition of Italian masterpieces from the Pinacoteca Tosio Martinengo, documented and completed by this catalog, is a very special event for Brescian culture and, we believe, for the city of Portland.

It is an opportunity to proudly exhibit a significant part of Brescia's rich artistic heritage. This astonishing selection of works comes from an important gallery established in the nineteenth century as a result of bequests from noble collectors, subsequently enriched by the municipality.

The exhibition continues on from other events featuring the city's artistic heritage. These have included presentations of great Italian masters, from Titian to Raphael, and the remarkable series entitled The splendor of art, with masterpieces by Monet, Gauguin, Van Gogh and Millet, visited by hundreds of thousands of art lovers.

A select part of the Brescian collections is now crossing the ocean to present the American public with a rational summary of north Italian art between the sixteenth and eighteenth centuries, with a particularly emphasis on Brescian masters. These are not so well known to the wider public but are familiar to art historians, who have rescued them from the oblivion they risked by not having "a metropolitan city as a theatre", as noted in the eighteenth century.

The event is a further example of the commitment to specialist temporary exhibitions and profitable cultural exchanges with other important international galleries. The works in the civic Pinacoteca–the "Sistine chapel of the Lombards", in the words of the great art historian Roberto Longhi–can in this way expand what is offered by our city museum, itself a symbol of Brescian culture and identity.

The exceptional nature of the pieces on display documents Brescia's "originality" in Italian art and reveals the precious nature of its collections, among the most interesting in Europe. An extraordinary range of paintings will now be visible for the first time in the United States at the Portland Art Museum. They begin with Renaissance works by Ferramola and an unknown Brescian artist, which once adorned the city's palazzi in the fifteenth century, and extraordinarily vivid sixteenth-century works painted by Moretto, Romanino, Savoldo, Lattanzio Gambara and Luca Mombello to embellish churches and private mansions.

There are then seventeenth-century works by Francesco Paglia and the Arcimboldesque painter Antonio Rasio, and scintillating works from the eighteenth century by Antonio Cifrondi and Giacomo Ceruti, called Pitochetto, documenting everyday life in the city on the eve of the Age of Enlightenment. The exhibition provides an excursion through different schools and periods, in which art reflects the separations and continuations dictated by history and by the cultural sensitivity of client and painter amid the fascinating overall history of Italian painting.

Paolo Corsini
Mayor of Brescia

This exhibition continues the association begun some years ago between Linea d'ombra and the Portland Art Museum. Last year this resulted in the presentation of some fine masterpieces from the American museum at the exhibition Monet, la Senna le ninfee, *at the Santa Giulia Museum, Brescia. This year a broad and significant selection of Italian paintings from between the sixteenth and eighteenth centuries is being shown at the Portland Art Museum. These are from the Pinacoteca Tosio Martinengo of Brescia, a city with which Linea d'ombra is involved in a long-term program of major exhibitions.*

Linea d'ombra had faith in this important project right from the start, eagerly arranging all organizational aspects, including publication of this catalog, and becoming its sponsor.

Sincere thanks to the editors of the catalog, Elena Lucchesi Ragni and Renata Stradiotti, and to Laura Rossi.

Thanks also to the exhibition curator, Penelope Hunter-Stiebel, who has reviewed the texts for an American readership.

Marco Goldin
General Director of Linea d'ombra

Contents

11   Discovering the Paintings of Brescia
Penelope Hunter-Stiebel

15   Discovering the City of Brescia

21   Masterpieces of Sixteenth-century Painting in Brescia
Mina Gregori

29   The Tosio Martinengo Pinacoteca.
Origins of the Collection and Brief Art Historical
Survey of the Paintings
Elena Lucchesi Ragni, Renata Stradiotti

39   Giacomo Ceruti in Brescia and the "Padernello Cycle"
Francesco Frangi

49   **Catalog**

151   Painters' Profiles

157   General Bibliography
Anna Alberti

167   Photo Credits

Discovering the Paintings of Brescia

Penelope Hunter-Stiebel

Discovering the paintings preserved in the museums of Brescia one realizes that something uniquely beautiful was created in this regional center again and again and again. Since the Renaissance the work of artists born in the region has been supplemented by those pausing to fill commissions, or settling in this city along the main east-west route across northern Italy. Their paintings on canvas or panel or in fresco have shaped a unique artistic heritage that has escaped attention due to the city's reputation as a modern industrial center. The legacy, however, has not been lost on generations of art historians who have argued over the personalities, themes, styles, and the crosscurrents of influence, in an effort to define the ineffable qualities particular to painting in Brescia. In the mid nineteenth century English connoisseurs became enthusiastic about Renaissance painting in northern Italy. An important representation of the school was assembled for the National Gallery in London by the purchases of the museum's first directors and the donations of distinguished private collectors. Still the artists' names remain unfamiliar to the general public. Michael Kimmelman, reviewing the exhibition *Painters of Reality: the Legacy of Leonardo and Caravaggio in Lombardy* at the Metropolitan Museum of Art, (*NY Times*, May 28, 2004) wrote of the Lombard artists, many of whom are featured here, "How many of these names ring bells? After you see what they have done, I bet you'll remember them…"

An art of fusion
The art of Brescia could be characterized as one of fusion. Its geographic location positioned it between two poles of Renaissance art: Milan where Leonardo da Vinci had such impact, and Venice, home to Titian, the international art celebrity of the following generation. Brescia was culturally linked to both. Although it became part of the mainland empire of the Venetian Republic in 1426, Brescia's churches remained under the archdiocese of Milan. Commerce and industry, including the mining of iron ore and the manufacture of arms and armor, provided a solid base of support for public and private commissions of art. Local artists were exposed to the latest in artistic innovations as they traveled, studied and competed successfully for commissions elsewhere. They knew the works of Netherlandish and German artists in originals as well as prints. Dürer painted a major altarpiece in Venice which had enormous impact on local artists. Even Alessandro Bonvicino, who was so totally identified with his native city that he was dubbed Moretto da Brescia, worked on commissions in Milan as well as other towns of

the Venetian state. For the composition of his monumental Pentecost altarpiece, he drew on Raphael's Vatican frescoes, which he would have known through engravings, as well as Titian's *Pentecost* altarpiece in Venice. The essays and entries in this catalog reference the massive amount of art historical literature fueled by the effort to analyze the compound influences absorbed in the paintings of Brescia.

Portraits

For the visitor to this exhibition, an introduction to the art of Brescia comes from the sixteenth-century gentlemen portrayed with riveting realism by Moretto and Moroni. The term "speaking likeness" comes to mind as we stand before people who lived more than four centuries ago, yet communicate to us directly through their portraits. Scholars have not yet found their names so we must take them as people of obvious and penetrating intelligence, be they nobles or men of letters, and wonder at the sophistication and skill of painters whose keen observation of detail brought an immediacy that was altogether new to their time. Our admiration echoes that of other sixteenth-century artists, including the great Titian, who commended Moroni for portraits of "true and natural likeness".

Frescoes

Murals in the demanding medium of fresco challenged the greatest artists of the Italian Renaissance. Michelangelo triumphed despite the rigors of painting the Sistine ceiling in small patches of wet plaster, but Leonardo failed in his experiment with a dry-wall alternative for the *Last Supper* which began to disintegrate almost immediately. Normally we can only experience the qualities of fresco by traveling to seek out surviving examples *in situ*. We may find religious imagery on the walls and ceilings of churches but we rarely discover the frescoes of secular subjects that embellished private palaces. In the sixteenth century frescoes animated the exteriors as well as the interiors of public and private buildings in Brescia. This exhibition brings us rare and precious elements by Brescia's masters of the medium detached from crumbling palace walls and preserved in the city's museum. Ferramola's imaginative narratives and Gambara's virtuoso classicism offer a taste of the refinement and quality of life enjoyed by prosperous residents of the city in the Renaissance.

Religious art

Italian artists translated the intensity of religious sentiment in the sixteenth-century into pictorial terms. They used their best efforts of skill and invention for the commissions of monumental altarpieces in major churches that were the source of fame and financial reward. But they also conveyed the potence of personal piety that many shared with their clients in the smaller format of pictures for devotional use. Great religious images were produced in Brescia from Romanino's *Christ Carrying the Cross*, a searing portrayal of pain which hung in Brescia's hospital, to Moretto's sublime *Penetecost* painted for the church of San Giuseppe. The two paintings evoke the experiences of compassion and exaltation that were central to church teaching and religious practice.

Decorative cycles

The seventeenth and eighteenth centuries saw the decline of the mainland empire of Venice as the Republic's attention turned to naval battles with the Turks. While Brescia's outlying territories suffered the ravages of foreign troops, the well-fortified city with its flourishing armaments industry sustained continued art production. Suites of large canvases depicting allegorical subjects became the fashionable idiom of decoration for grand residences. This exhibition presents complete cycles that allow us to appreciate the original concept of related compositions, rather than seeing just the individual canvases that have found their way to museums abroad. The most surprising are Ceruti's paintings of common people and beggars portrayed with empathy and respect as they look out at us from their hardscrabble lives. Their provenance goes back to the noble Avogadro family of Brescia. The cycle was not installed in private rooms of their residences where subjects for moral edification might be expected, but rather in reception rooms hung with other paintings, including grand portraits by Moretto and Moroni, for guests to admire. The increasing number of paintings recorded in the Avogadro inventories over the course of the eighteenth century reveal that they were avid art collectors. The explanation for Ceruti's unusual cycle, may be that his patrons recognized a contemporary talent on the level of the "Old Masters" they were acquiring, and by this commission sought to give him the scope to portray the humanity of the subjects he most cared about.

An international exchange

The extraordinary opportunity for Portland, Oregon to have the loan of thirty-five paintings from Brescia results from an international exchange under the aegis of Linea d'ombra. Its director, Marco Goldin, requested the loan from the Portland Art Museum of a Renoir and two Monets (including the most beloved work in the museum's collection, the large *Waterlilies* of 1914-15) for his 2004 exhibition in Brescia, *Monet, la Senna, le ninfee. Il grande fiume e il nuovo secolo.* Fortuitously the construction schedule for Portland's new Center for Contemporary and Modern Art required that the Impressionists be retired from view for several months prior to their reinstallation in the new wing, making it possible for them to travel. As Portland's curator of European Art, I welcomed Linea d'ombra's invitation to come to Brescia to work with Dotteressa Renata Stradiotti, the Director of the Museums of Brescia, on an exhibition that would present the riches of her museum to a new audience in the Pacific Northwest. After months of refining the concept and loan list and gaining the approval of the administration of the Italian Ministry of Culture we can proudly present the exhibition that this publication documents. It could not have happened without the initiative of Marco Goldin, the leadership of John Buchanan, Director of the Portland Art Museum until earlier this year, the enthusiastic support of Brescia's mayor, Paolo Corsini, and the expertise of Dottoressa Stradiotti, assisted by Laura Rossi at the Museums of Brescia. In a record three months Silvia Zancanella, editor for Linea d'ombra, working with translator David Graham, has created the catalog drawing on the scholarship of leading Italian specialists. Most of all the dedication and tireless efforts of Caterina Barbini and Zaira Bellet of Linea d'ombra made possible this unique international exchange.

Discovering the City of Brescia

Brescia is in the heart of tourist country and attracts millions of people each year, thanks to its location, its tradition of hospitality, its infrastructure and the beauty of its landscape: from the mountains of its three valleys to the shores of its lakes. The historical, artistic and cultural wealth of the area is an added value expressed by its museums and by its art, natural beauty and typical food and drink.

The importance of industrial production in this city on the Alpine foothills has until recently diverted attention from its artistic and historic treasures. The city may be described as "beautiful and brooding; the proud custodian of its artistic beauty, just waiting to be discovered". Indeed, its ancient buildings reveal astonishing layers, starting from the important Roman remains around the Piazza del Foro (the Republican sanctuary, the capitolium, the theatre and the basilica) near the Santa Giulia museum.

A fortified castle known as "The falcon of Italy" overlooks the city from the top of the Cidneo hill. Ancient sources (Livy, Pliny, Polybius and Strabo) write of Brescia as *caput Cenomanorum*, the capital of the Cenis Galls who settled on the slopes of the Cidneo around the fifth century BC. The city's Latin name recalls these circumstances and the people's Celtic language ("Brixia" derives from "brig", which means hill or mount).

The hill has been the site of important buildings since Roman times. The entire fourteenth-century keep built by the Viscontis, with its crenellated wall and two circular towers, incorporates a temple from the first century AD, which is perfectly aligned with the capitolium and the forum. From the third century BC Brescia was a loyal and powerful ally to Rome, and an important trading partner. After the fall of the Roman Empire, the city was for two centuries one of the most important Lombard dukedoms, which gave the realm two kings: Rotari and Desiderio.

The growing need for defenses and the succession of foreign rulers, primarily Venice, led to the entire hill being turned into a formidable fortress. The castle expanded in still legible concentric circles over a period dating from the middle ages to the 1600s.

Today the fortress complex retains enormous interest as it houses the Museum of the Risorgimento and the Weapons Museum surrounded by the natural beauty of a splendid terrace overlooking the city.

The Museum of the Risorgimento exhibits documents and artifacts from the period between the French Revolution (1789) and the capture of Rome (1870). It is in the

View of Brescia from Cidneo hill, at bottom right the Santa Giulia complex, above the Duomo Nuovo and the Torre del Broletto

The Castle on Cidneo hill, at bottom the porticoes on the east side of the Piazza della Loggia and the Torre di Porta Bruciata

The Tempio Capitolino, built in 73 AD by the emperor Vespasian

Grande Miglio building (built in 1597 as a grain storehouse) and has been housed in the castle since 1959. The period from the Congress of Vienna to the 10 Days of 1849, when Brescia rose up against the Austrians and earned the title "the Lioness of Italy", is particularly well documented. The city was also one of the most generous suppliers of Garibaldi's Mille expedition; as a consequence there are many important displays relating to Garibaldi in the museum.

The Weapons Museum is one of the largest of its kind in Europe and occupies the keep. The collection consists of 580 pieces from a total of 1090 artifacts collected by Luigi Marzoli, an industrialist from Palazzolo sull'Oglio, who donated them to the city in 1965. This important collection traces the development of the arms industry (in which Brescia has always been involved) between the fifteenth and sixteenth centuries. The collection features numerous pieces of fine armor, 100-odd helmets, short and long bayonets, about 50 rifles, 90 pistols, 15 cannons and 150 firearm accessories.

Brescia offers numerous itineraries, which the city has discovered and is rediscovering as it upgrades its hidden treasures: historic sites, churches, museums, *palazzi* and cloisters, with works by Foppa, Romanino, Moretto and Savoldo. The Pinacoteca Tosio Martinengo houses an important collection of works by these and many other artists. The three squares of the city center express the "local color" in stone and marble.

First and foremost of these is the Piazza della Loggia, built by the magistrate Foscari in 1433. It is magnificently set off by the Loggia (the finest example of Renaissance architecture in Brescia), the Palazzo Notarile, the Casa Vender, the building known as the prison, the arcades and clock tower, the Loggetta and the Old and New Palazzi del Monte di Pietà on whose facade there is a stone with Roman inscriptions.

The Piazza del Duomo, now the Piazza Paolo VI in honor of the Brescian pope, Giovan Battista Montini, provides the "wings" of a spectacular stage setting, overlooked by the Rotonda of the Duomo Vecchio, the Duomo Nuovo and the Broletto.

Built in the eleventh century, the Duomo Vecchio is an exceptional example of Italian Romanesque architecture. It is one of the few examples of a circular Romanesque church, based on the model of the Holy Sepulcher in Jerusalem. The dome covering the vast central space rests on eight enormous arches supported by pillars. The Rotonda contains the marble sarcophagus of Berardo Maggi. The Crypt of Saint Filastrio beneath the chancel is part of the ancient basilica and still has the remains of some of its mosaics. There are some important works by Romanino and a magnificent organ by Antegnati (1536) in the Duomo Vecchio. It also houses the Treasure of the Holy Saints and the Field Cross. The latter was once a memorial to religious devotion and to the proud opposition of the Lombard towns to Federico Barbarossa.

The Duomo Nuovo stands right in the middle of the east side of the square. Its construction began in 1604 on the site of the early Christian basilica of San Pietro de Dom (fifth-sixth century). It has a solemn, imposing facade and a Greek-cross interior with three aisles and central frescoed dome. Its many important works include the *Nuptials*, the *Visitation* and the *Birth of the Virgin* by Romanino, and Moretto's *Sacrifice of Isaac*.

The Broletto (12th–13th centuries) is undoubtedly one of the most elegant municipal palaces in Lombardy. Over the centuries it has undergone many transformations and extensions, but retains the essence of its original Romanesque style. Its name derives

The Duomo Vecchio or Rotonda (ca. XI century) based on the Holy Sepulcher in Jerusalem

The courtyard of the Palazzo Broletto (XIII century), the dome of the Duomo Nuovo and the Torre del Pegol or del Popolo in the center

from its construction on the site of an orchard, or "brolo". The broad central courtyard features an eighteenth-century fountain and the impressive Torre del Pegol, a tower of Botticino stone standing almost 54 meters high.

The Piazza della Vittoria is an example of the 1930's Neo-Classicism of the architect Piacentini, whose work can be found in many Italian cities, from Genoa to Bari. Innaugurated in 1932, it replaced an entire working-class neighborhood in the heart of the city. It is overlooked by the Post Office, the brick Torrione (the "Skyscraper") and buildings entirely clad in marble.

The many important churches include some genuine architectural and artistic gems. In particular, Santa Maria dei Miracoli, in Corso Martiri della Libertà, which has been declared part of the Unesco's "world heritage" because of the beautiful sculptures on its Botticino stone facade. It dates from 1487 and was built on a site previously graced by a reputedly miraculous painting of the Blessed Virgin.

An itinerary from one to another of Brescia's many churches offers a fascinating tour of art and history: from San Faustino Maggiore, dedicated to the patron saints of the city, to Santa Maria del Carmine, with its bare brick facade and on to Sant'Agata, San Giuseppe, Santa Maria della Pace, the sanctuary of Madonna delle Grazie, San Francesco d'Assisi, San Clemente and San Cristo (the last covered in a wealth of frescoes). The stupendous *Averoldi Polyptych* painted by Titian between 1520 and 1522 can be admired in the church of Saints Nazaro and Celso, along with other works. The Sacramental Chapel in San Giovanni has the finest example of Brescian painting from the 1500s, with the "competition" between Romanino (left-hand wall) and Moretto (right-hand wall), whose works depicting stories from the Bible and the Gospels "challenge one another". All these, and others, are treasure houses of art, faith, culture and tradition that deserve an attentive visit.

Inner courtyard of the Palazzo Martinengo da Barco

The Nuns Choir from the south. In the foreground, an arcade of the west cloister

The Pinacoteca Tosio Martinengo

"The Pinacoteca Tosio Martinengo was set up in 1906 by merging the Tosio Gallery, bequeathed to the city in 1846 by Count Paolo Tosio, and the Martinengo Gallery, opened after 1887 in the *palazzo* donated to the city by Count F. Leonardo Martinengo da Barco to house paintings of various origins" according to the account of the art gallery in Piazza Moretto by the distinguished art historian, Professor Gaetano Panazza.

The gallery's 25 rooms contain works by some of the leading masters of the fifteenth- and sixteenth-century Brescian school: Vincenzo Foppa, Giovanni Girolamo Savoldo, Alessandro Bonvicino, called Moretto and Girolamo Romani, called Romanino. It also boasts artists from other periods, such as Lorenzo Lotto, Giacomo Ceruti, Andrea Celesti, Maffei, Civerchio, Palma Giovane, Paolo Veneziano, some Flemish painters and other truly great names, such as Raphael. The main nucleus consists of works by three major sixteenth-century Brescian artists: Savoldo, Romanino and Moretto. Savoldo is well represented by the *Adoration of the Shepherds*, a fine example of this artist who managed to give every work in his limited production a rare unity of style, with a plastic sense of form accentuated by light effects anticipating those of Caravaggio. Romanino's work documents his Venetian chromatism–deriving from the school of Giorgione and Titian–enlivened by his personal imagination. Moretto's work is calmer, more serene and infused with intimism and piety. Throughout his career he retained a balance between the tradition of Foppa, Lombard realism and festive Venetian painting.

But the Pinacoteca Tosio Martinengo encompasses more than Renaissance painting: there are also important eighteenth-century and Romantic paintings, along with numerous prints and drawings by important artists.

The Museum of Santa Giulia

The Museo della Città occupies an area of around 14,000 square meters in a monastic complex of Lombard origins, making it unique in Europe. It offers a journey through the history, art and spirituality of Brescia from prehistoric times to the present day. The Benedictine convent of San Salvatore-Santa Giulia was built by the Lombard king Desiderio and his wife Ansa in 753. It played an important religious, political and economic role, even after the Lombards' defeat at the hands of Charlemagne. The dramatic story of Ermengarda, daughter of King Desiderio and the rejected wife of Charlemagne, recounted by the poet and novelist Alessandro Manzoni in his tragedy *Adelchi* (1822), took place here.

The warp and weft of different epochs form a source of surprising discoveries in this site of interwoven historical memories. Built over Roman structures, a Roman road and dwellings with mosaic floors, it includes the Lombard basilica of San Salvatore and its crypt, the Romanesque oratory of Santa Maria in Solario, the Nuns Choir, the sixteenth-century church of Santa Giulia and the Renaissance cloisters. It is a natural museum of the city and should be the starting point of any tour of Brescia.

The museum is defined by the close link between the architectural showcase and the objects it displays. At present, the Santa Giulia presents around 11,000 items: Celtic

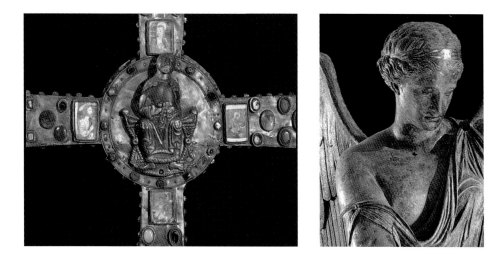

The *Cross of Desiderio* (obverse, detail with *Christ Enthroned*, a fine example of medieval gold work (end of VIII century)

The *Winged Victory*, famous bronze sculpture from the first century AD, found in a wall cavity in the Capitolium and now on display in the Santa Giulia Museo della Città

The Domus of Dionysis. The triclinio with a framed image of Dionysis and the panther

artifacts, helmets and breastplates, Roman portraits and bronzes, Lombard relics, funeral chests, frescoes and collections of objects of art from medieval times to the eighteenth century. The symbol of the city is the winged Victory. This enormous bronze, which recent studies have revealed to be four centuries older than originally thought, is a Greek original of Aphrodite and was intended for the sanctuary at Rhodes. It arrived in Rome as war booty and was then donated to Brixia, where it was converted into a representation of Victory by the addition of wings.

Extensive archaeological excavations have brought to light the "Domus dell'Ortaglia": a splendid residential complex from Roman times (1st century BC–4th century AD) with around 40 richly decorated rooms. Transformation of the *domus* into a museum in 2003 has not only enriched the visit to the Roman town in the Santa Giulia Museum, but offers an exciting "immersion" into the neighborhoods of Brixia. Along paths following the ancient roads, visitors can take in the space of the courtyards, the volumes of the rooms, the mosaic paving that is closely related to the frescoed walls, and overlook the green spaces (reproduced in the exterior viridarium).

The treasury of Santa Giulia has been relocated in the Romanesque oratory of Santa Maria in Solario where lavishly decorated objects of great devotional value, most notably the Cross of Desiderio, are surrounded by sixteenth-century frescoes under a star-studded dome.

A key element of the monastery architecture is the Nuns Choir; a masterpiece of Renaissance Brescian art, restored to its original state and adorned with one of the most significant pictorial cycles in the city by Floriano Ferramola and Paolo da Caylina il Giovane. The wealth and importance of the monastery are confirmed by the decorations and liturgical ornaments of the medieval church of San Salvatore, with ancient marbles, decorative stuccoes on the arches of the naves and frescoes that mark the centuries of the monastery's history.

A new addition to the international circuit, the museum was opened in 1999 after decades of studies, excavations, preservation and restoration work, thanks to the combined efforts of the city council, the CAB Foundation and the Banco di Brescia.

Masterpieces of Sixteenth-century Painting in Brescia

Mina Gregori

Brescia was specifically addressed by the scholars Lanzi, Crowe, Cavalcaselle and Adolfo Venturi in their definition of Italian art centers as schools, with further contributions made by Morelli, Rio, Berenson and Longhi. Such definition, though undoubtedly useful, is now no longer regarded as appropriate because of its academic roots.

Brescia was placed within the Venetian school, from which it was later differentiated by Cavalcaselle (1871). The distinctive position and importance of Brescian artists already seemed clear, however, to Lanzi (1795–96): "excellent painters, but little known because they had no metropolitan city as a theatre".

Romanino, Moretto and Savoldo dominated in the first half of the sixteenth century. They were exponents of Vasari's "modern manner" and, as such, "real" people, emerging with strong individual characteristics outside the confines of the medieval workshop still current in the fifteenth century. Leaving aside Foppa and the style of Civerchio and Ferramola, who Cavalcaselle recalls in his *History of Painting in North Italy* (1871), these three painters of the subsequent generation assimilated Venetian painting innovations.

The first to move in this direction was Girolamo Romanino, who was only slightly older than Moretto and had survived the vicissitudes of war. He had worked in outlying towns like Tavernola, where Brescian political exiles had taken refuge, and in Padua, where two of his masterpieces can still be seen. His *Lamentation*, painted in 1510 for San Lorenzo in Brescia, was taken from the church at the beginning of the nineteenth century and a century later bought by the Venice Accademia. The panels from the main altar of San Cristo, dating from 1511, met the same fate (they are now in Kassel and a Milan collection). The painter was in Brescia in 1516, and his big altarpiece signed in that year is still on the main altar of the church of San Francesco. It develops the pattern of the Padua altarpiece (now in the collection of the civic museums), with a new, majestic breadth confirming his Venetian roots and the love of splendid, sumptuous fabrics shared by the Veneto and Flanders.

In the nineteenth century Moretto was represented by a larger number of works on public display in the churches of Brescia, most of them now transferred to the Pinacoteca Tosio Martinengo. He had enjoyed greater respect than Romanino, from

Alessandro Bonvicino called Moretto da Brescia, *Last Supper* (in lunette), *Elijah Comforted by the Angel* (in painting at left), *The Gathering of the Manna* (in painting at right), Brescia, church of San Giovanni Evangelista, Santissimo Sacramento chapel

21

Alessandro Bonvicino called Moretto da Brescia, *St Faustinus and St Jovita*, Lovere (Bergamo) Basilica di Santa Maria in Valvendra

the time of Vasari (1568), ("But Alessandro Moretto was more skilled than he"), an opinion that was to be shared by Cavalcaselle, undoubtedly due to Moretto's noble and unpretentious classicism.

Moretto was the object of enthusiastic discoveries and penetrating interpretations throughout the nineteenth century, starting with Lanzi. The great Marches connoisseur found him "so full of enticements that some enthusiasts have been to Brescia with the sole intention of enjoying them", He observed that "compunction, compassion and charity itself are clearly apparent in the religious subjects". His interpretation has been confirmed by Guazzoni (1981), whose studies on the painter's active involvement in the Scuola del Sacramento attached to the cathedral have countered Longhi's secular reading. A contribution to Moretto's emergence in the context of sixteenth-century Brescia was made by Morelli (1857 and 1865, see Agosti, 1985) and Rio (1861), who also noted ethical and religious values in his painting. These merged with the artistic qualities and appealed to thinking in the Restoration era. Morelli and his friends working in Lombardy defined a connection between the Brescian painter and the early artists, who were considered the height of value and taste from the 1850s thanks to Ruskin, and sought after for the National Gallery of London.

In a brilliant stroke of insight, Cavalcaselle recognized Moretto's hand alongside that of Ferramola in the organ shutters in Lovere, which were originally in the Duomo Vecchio of Brescia.

The participation of both Romanino and Moretto from 1521 in the important commission of decorating the Santissimo Sacramento chapel in San Giovanni Evangelista shows the similar esteem they enjoyed in Brescia at that time. But Moretto was to find greater consensus. Current assessments of the artists, however, like those of the nineteenth century, are hampered by the absence of two very important works painted by Romanino in the 1520s and early 1530s, removed in the early nineteenth century. These are the Sant'Alessandro polyptych and the *Lamentation*. The former, now in the National Gallery of London, was taken from the main altar around 1790 and its panels sold by the Averoldi in the 1850s. The latter, highly praised by seventeenth- and eighteenth-century writers, was taken from the church of Santi Faustino e Giovita in 1800, to the Kaiser-Friedrich museum and unfortunately destroyed in World War II. Finding the Romanino of these years requires a visit to San Giovanni Evangelista and to Santa Maria in Calchera to see the *Mass of St Apollonius*. This clearly shows his move toward the cursive, communicative style launched by Vincenzo Foppa in Milan, and which had another closer precedent in the similar treatment of Lorenzo Lotto's *Vestiture of St Bridget* in Trescore. The Brescian took up its ideas for an altarpiece, which also had iconic requirements.

Two wonderful portraits by Savoldo and Moretto in the Pinacoteca Tosio Martinengo compel consideration of the meaning and importance of portrait painting in Brescia in the first half of the sixteenth century, and its constant differentiation from that of Venice. Giorgionesque moods are enhanced and extended by psychological inquiries that could only have been suggested by the great Milanese lesson of Leonardo's *Last Supper*. This tendency may be ascribed to the leadership of Lorenzo Lotto who was in Bergamo from 1513. The Brescian style can be traced from the youthful *Last Supper* in Padua (civic museums) by Romanino, datable to 1513. He acknowledged Leonardo in his choice of subject and signs of Leonardo's influence are evident in the objects arranged on the table and the projection of their shadow in Romanino's subsequent *Last Supper* altarpiece in Montichiari. The ill-tempered spleen expressed in some of the heads was a characteristic that the Brescian was never to abandon. It is interesting that a similar effect can be found in Lotto's portraits. The simplest explanation is that a relationship developed between the two painters; the more complex one suggests that a sympathy existed between Romanino and the Venetian, who had recently returned from the Marches region, though initially they may not have had any direct contacts. The restiveness of character that Romanino soon transferred to portraiture reveals an investigation into the psyche based on Giorgionesque and Leonardesque elements he may have received indirectly through other artists.

The persistence of these tendencies in Brescia is confirmed in the Leonardo- and Lotto-inspired moods of the *Last Supper* commissioned from Moretto for the Sacramento chapel, and in its predecessor, the full-length *Portrait of a Nobleman*, now in London, painted in 1526. It is further exemplified by the *Man with a Flute*

Girolamo Romani called
Romanino, *The Mass of
St Gregory* (in lunette), *Raising
of Lazarus* (in painting at left),
Supper in the House of the Pharisee
(in painting at right) Brescia,
church of San Giovanni
Evangelista, Santissimo
Sacramento chapel

Girolamo Romani called
Romanino, *Last Supper*
Montichiari (Brescia), Duomo

by Savoldo, from the 1520s, and the later *Portrait* by Moretto, which retains its psychological edge. (Both are exhibited here.) The autonomy of art in Brescia was evident in paintings in the churches of the city and nearby towns. As in other critical cases in the development of Italian art, church commissions provided the means of expressing innovative artistic and human values. The Pinacoteca has several such works by Vincenzo Foppa, including the Mercanzia altarpiece and the famous Orzinovi standard. This Brescian painter left a legacy to the city in his frescoes and panel paintings, and also in years of teaching. After a long period of work in Milan, in December of 1489 the city council of Brescia invited him to return to run a painting and architecture school.

Foppa passed on to the painters of subsequent generations a feeling for nature revealed by the study of light as an empirical element. This was at odds with the unifying conception of humanism introduced and adopted in Padua. Instead of an even universal light Foppa preferred to evoke the tone of evening. He achieved this with a grey priming of the painting surface, a practice taken up by his followers. He then worked up a low base tone and applied intensively flamboyant colors rather than the mixed, harmonious ones of Venice. The painter introduced principles that ran counter to the anthropocentric concept of Humanism and made Brescia into a centre of advanced "trends" that would eventually be fully developed by Caravaggio. Foppa's painting humbly proposed an alternative view of the world and its phenomena through light, rather than the Renaissance focus on the actions of man. The Brescian set the foundations for Lombard Naturalism. Starting from a different conception of the world and of vision, learned from the Flemish, this went beyond the frontiers of humanism and was necessarily also a philosophy. Moretto continued Foppa's use of light and color, prompting Cavalcaselle to note his "low greenish adumbration of the flesh", which erroneously reminded him of Sebastiano del Piombo.

The sequence of Moretto's altarpieces in the Pinacoteca Tosio Martinengo allows his return to his Brescian roots to be traced, starting from the *Standard of the Holy Crosses*, which betrays his Venetian background and familiarity with Lorenzo Lotto. They document an artist who, although belonging to the Venetian-based "modern manner", complemented this with a submissive, albeit constructed, classicism, probably partly influenced by the Erasmus legacy in Brescia, along with the more profound and discreet principles of Foppa.

An interest in nature is apparent in the *Moses and the Burning Bush*, where the bush takes up most of the picture. In the altarpiece with *St Anthony of Padua between Saints Anthony Abbot and Nicholas of Tolentino*, the light filters into the canopy of the niche, while the inventions of "seen" rather than designed form in the hands of the main figures may have influenced Caravaggio. In the *Supper at Emmaus* the dense, pre-Caravaggesque shadows define a context that moves from the solemnity of the columns in the background to the touching domesticity of the figures in the foreground.

Other notable examples of human values brought to life by deft shadowing can be seen in the *Nativity with St Jerome and a Donor Monk* from Santa Maria delle Grazie, the *Madonna and Child with St Nicholas of Bari and the Pupils of the Grammarian Rovelli*, previously in Santa Maria dei Miracoli, and the *Ecce Homo and the Angel*, previously in the Duomo Vecchio. The latter recalls the pathos of the great Flemish painters and German engravers.

The altarpiece depicting the *Virgin and Child with the Infant St John in Glory*, from the church of Sant'Eufemia, is a supreme and much admired example of the colorist splendor achieved by Moretto. Light defines the figures in sharp optical relief with clear contrasting colors that stand out within the perspective construction. The brilliant rendering of the floral silk brocades and embroideries derives from the Flemish tradition through Foppa and Romanino.

The accuracy of Moretto's optical analysis is apparent in his use of light. The young Titian had made subtle experiments with silken fabrics, which reflect the light, especially on the edges of pleats and the brightness of black, but these had soon been replaced in Venice by a preference for homogenizing blends of pigments. Moretto however continued the earlier techniques incorporating them in the stillness of his religious meditations such as in the Paitone *Virgin* and the splendid garments of the *St Justine* in Vienna. He also used them to achieve the preciousness appropriate to holy images and ceremonies, such as in the *Coronation of the Virgin* in Santi Nazaro e Celso and in the *Virgin Enthroned with Saints* in Sant'Andrea, Bergamo. He even brought out hints of engraving in the silvered light of the Raphaelesque *Massacre of the Innocents* in San Giovanni Evangelista.

Moretto's approach to visual phenomenon differed from that of the Venetians,

Alessandro Bonvicino called Moretto da Brescia, *Apparition of the Virgin to Filippo Viotti*, Paitone (Brescia), Santuario

and was adopted by painters in the cities of the Venetian mainland (Cavalcaselle noted that Paolo Veronese used Brescian adaptations of the Venetian style).

In Cremona, too, prior to Caravaggio, Antonio Campi looked to the Naturalist discoveries developed in Brescia when embarking on his campaign against Mannerism.

Already in the 1510's Romanino anticipated Moretto in his interest in showing the effect of light on folds in drapery. This can be seen in the Kassel panels and the Tavernola fresco, and again in the small altarpiece of Salò cathedral, dated to just before 1520. He then delighted in the splendor of the Virgin's floral cape in the *Marriage of the Virgin* in San Giovanni Evangelista and in the broad patterns on the clothing in the *Portrait of a Nobleman* in Budapest, shining like a resplendent cuirass.

Later, in the 1540s, Romanino exquisitely modulated the play of light on larger expanses of satin in paintings like the *Virgin and Child* in the diocesan museum of Brescia and the *Marriage of St Catherine* in Memphis. He was even moved to embellish inappropriate contexts, like his depictions of *Christ Carrying the Cross* with a silk cloak in the Pinacoteca's tondo included in this exhibition and in the fine canvas formerly in the Averoldi home and now in the Brera. The *Nativity* in the Pinacoteca is from this group of works. The attention to surfaces on the Virgin's broad, symbolically silver-white silk cape, which may seem no more than decorative enhancement, is actually the result of investigations into the nature and action of light, which were to be furthered by artists who developed Naturalism in the seventeenth century. In this phase Romanino's work was more in tune with that of Gerolamo Savoldo. Indeed, the fine notation of the stitching in the cape of the *Nativity* is a direct citation of the celebrated *St Mary Magdalene Approaching the Sepulcher* by Savoldo, probably from the version now in London.

There was a close relationship between Romanino and Moretto, working in Brescia and the surrounding region, and Gerolamo Savoldo, the third major figure of sixteenth-century Brescian painting, who settled in Venice after a period of travels. Their common Lombard roots, reinforced by their recognizably similar intentions and contacts, are particularly evident in the innovations that came to Lombardy through Savoldo's works, as in the case of the *Magdalene*. Savoldo was the main interpreter of night scenes, an example of which is Romanino's *St Mathew* in the Sacramento chapel in San Giovanni Evangelista, dating from the 1540s. This painting conforms with the unsettled and ever changing course of Romanino's career. It was probably inspired by four paintings by Savoldo which were admiringly described by Vasari as "four very fine night and fire paintings". Originally in the Milan Mint, one of them is identified as the *St Mathew and the Angel* now in the Metropolitan Museum of New York.

The panel with the *Adoration of the Shepherds* by Savoldo, painted in 1540 for the Bargnani chapel in San Barnaba and now in the Pinacoteca, offered Brescia a different model. The dilapidated hut and the natural gesture of the shepherd taking off his hat particularize this portrayal of rustic life seen at dusk. The presence of the shepherds looking on from outside relates to Flemish iconography, but the work also

inspires other considerations, due to the existence of similar compositions in San Giobbe in Venice and in Terlizzi. The practice of copying compositions, which was evident in Savoldo's *Magdalene* and would recur with Caravaggio. This also would explain the loose execution and numerous pentimenti in Savoldo's *Adoration*.

Romanino is admirably represented in the Pinacoteca by the big altarpiece painted for the main altar in San Domenico. Faced with the difficult task of depicting the subject of the Virgin crowned by the Trinity observed by a large number of saints grouped around the patron of the work, the artist dispensed with the architectural framing devices used by Moretto to place his figures in an uninterrupted Veneto landscape and endow them with a variety of attitudes and expressions. The sumptuous clothing in contrasting colors worn by Saints Faustinus and Jovita who kneel in the foreground were surely Caravaggio's inspiration in his painting of card-sharps now in Fort Worth. Romanino undoubtedly intended to astonish with his masterful imitation of nature in the bright shining surfaces of the greaves and bracers of the armor visible under the garments.

Romanino's experiments and breadth of interest cannot be fully appreciated without proper study of his frescoes, a highly valued technical specialty which, unlike Moretto, he used often. The detached frescoes from the Rodengo abbey now in the Pinacoteca offer fine examples of his "intellect" and "honesty of brush" admired by Lanzi. He emphasized Romanino's "range of action" his "energy of expression" and his "possession of art extended to the treatment of any subject". The Rodengo frescoes also show how Romanino developed his study of expressions and the fluidity of his narration over the years. The initial stimulus in the 1510s came through his acquaintance with Leonardo's model, the presence of Lorenzo Lotto in Bergamo, his own familiarity with the Cremona painters and his knowledge of German prints.

The solid draftsmanship underlying Romanino's painting was refined with the originally central-Italian technique of chiaroscuro in parallel and cross hatching. This had first been taken up by the Cremona painters, starting with Boccaccio Boccaccino, who had learnt it directly from Rome, and by the "anti-classical" movements in the north. Practiced by Romanino in Brescia, the technique can now also be quite clearly read in Moretto's *Saints Faustinus and Jovita on Horseback* after its cleaning, painted on the organ shutters at Lovere. It is not surprising that Romanino's vast activity as a draftsman distinguishes him from the other Brescia painters.

The skill of his draftsmanship can be seen in his *St Jerome Penitent* dating from 1516–17 in the Pinacoteca, where the same incisive and tormented line defines the scanty clothing of the saint and the rocks of the background. Moretto's friendship with the Cremona artist Altobello Melone is evident here. They had worked together in Bovezzo and Melone's work has at times been mistaken for Romanino's. So it is no surprise that Moretto was invited to appraise Melone's works in the nave of Cremona cathedral and, subsequently, in 1519, was chosen to continue the cycle of frescoes with the *Stories of the Passion*, following on from those of Gian Francesco Bembo and Melone. The opportunity to observe these closely during recent restoration work revealed his wonderful drafting matched with the richness of Venetian color, contrasting with the adjacent frescoes by the Cremona artists.

Romanino's fresco works show the new and restless mood he shared with itinerant artists like Amico Aspertini and Lorenzo Lotto in his decoration of the loggia and other rooms in the Buonconsiglio castle in 1531–32. Here the meeting with German culture explains his use of genre scenes, and profane subjects that were not to be fully adopted until the seventeenth century. Indeed his pictorial license deemed incompatible with the decoration was greeted with some reservation by the client, Bernardo Clesio, the prince bishop of Trent. The Val Camonica frescoes from the 1530s correspond to periodic returns home that were to conclude in his derisive treatment of ancient myths in the rooms of the Palazzi Averoldi and Lechi. These frescoes reveal the artistic and human development of his contrasting view of two different civilizations, with themes that are on one hand playful and vulgar, on the other tragic: the somber mountainous setting of the *Stories of Christ* in Pisogne and the disturbing evocation of the story told in the Book of Daniel at Breno. Romanino was long underrated because his work in fresco was alien to the formalist preferences of nineteenth-century critics, but recent reappraisals by Giovanni Testori and Alessandro Nova show his reputation is being restored.

The Tosio Martinengo Pinacoteca. Origins of the Collection and Brief Art Historical Survey of the Paintings

Elena Lucchesi Ragni, Renata Stradiotti

The Pinacoteca Tosio Martinengo in the Palazzo Martinengo da Barco was created in 1906 by merging the Tosio and Martinengo art galleries. The former was bequeathed to the city of Brescia in 1832 by Count Paolo Tosio (1775–1842), who had assembled a splendid collection of paintings, drawings, prints, glassware and ceramics in his family's *palazzo*. This sixteenth-century building was completely redesigned by Rodolfo Vantini in Neoclassical style and opened to the public in 1851.

In 1883 the city of Brescia then inherited the Martinengo family *palazzo* and its collections of rare books, codices, prints, scientific instruments and medals, from Count Francesco Leopardo Martinengo. The collection of early work was opened in this building in 1889, while the modern art section remained in the Palazzo Tosio.

In 1906 the two galleries were joined to form the Pinacoteca Tosio Martinengo in the Palazzo Martinengo da Barco. Along with the Tosio and Martinengo collections, this housed other nineteenth- and early twentieth-century bequests, works held on deposit, items from churches closed during the Napoleonic suppressions and detached frescoes from demolished buildings.

The Palazzo Martinengo da Barco was probably built by Count Ludovico in the early sixteenth century, incorporated some existing fourteenth-century buildings that can still be partially seen on the ground floor. Count Francesco Leopardo (namesake of the nineteenth-century donor) had the building renovated in the late sixteenth century. He built the Via Martinengo da Barco facade, with statues of Mars and Pallas by Andrea Paracca above its doorway, the inside doors and enclosed the loggia arcade on the floor above. The *palazzo* was further enlarged and remodeled in the eighteenth century. The grand staircase ceiling is decorated with the *Apotheosis of the Martinengo Family* by an unknown artist.

Some final renovations were carried out when the building was converted into a museum. Some old sections were demolished and Piazza Moretto was created, thereby also opening up the east wing, which was redesigned to match the south facade.

The monument to Moretto was erected on the fourth centenary of his birth, aligned with the doorway and entrance hall of the *palazzo*. Also visible from the garden behind, it links the city to the splendid heritage held in the museum.

The Pinacoteca currently contains paintings from the twelfth century to the eighteenth.

Brescian art was open to outside influences in the late Middle Ages and the four-

Anonymous, *St George Freeing the Princess from the Dragon* ca. 1450–60 (Inv. 114)

Vincenzo Foppa, *Madonna and Child with Saints Faustinus and Jovita*, ca. 1505–10 (Inv. 124)

teenth century. It therefore constantly incorporated innovations, which the unstable political situation of the times seems to have actually fostered. This is evident in the paintings from the city's churches and *palazzi*.

After the municipal rule of medieval times and the short reign of Bishop Berardo Maggi (1298–1308), Brescia was not powerful enough to maintain its independence and fell under the rule of the Visconti from 1337 to 1426, briefly interrupted by the Pandolfo Malatesta lordship from 1404 to 1421.

The painting of this period was influenced both by Venice and the Byzantine world, and by Giotto's frescoes in nearby Padua; there were also examples of the "courtly" style of Lombard origin.

The Brescia area was partly influenced by contemporary Venetian painting through the work of Paolo Veneziano. The Pinacoteca has several panels from a mid-fourteenth-century polyptych he painted showing *St John the Baptist, St Paul and two Holy Bishops*, originally in the monastery of Santi Cosma e Damiano. The Byzantine style is here enriched with Gothic elements, and by the bright, typically Venetian colors that stand out against the gold background.

Bright colors also distinguish the panel of *St George and the Dragon*, from the second half of the fifteenth century, originally in the church of San Giorgio. This panel shows late influences of an important artistic event that took place in Brescia in 1415–19: Pandolfo Malatesta commissioned Gentile da Fabriano to decorate his private chapel in the Palazzo Broletto. This has now been almost entirely lost. The fresco decoration was an extremely lavish, elegant example of International Gothic, which long influenced artistic development in the city. The unidentified northern Italian painter joined areas of gold, both in the background and on the plaster reliefs, with the realistic landscape details, showing a familiarity with Renaissance perspective studies.

The most fertile period of art in the city began with Vincenzo Foppa (ca. 1430–1515/16). He made a definitive break from the International Gothic tradition of northern Italy and introduced the Humanist-archeological innovations made in Padua. He was also aware of the perspective studies from central Italy, but interpreted these in a realistic way using somber colors and a cold light. The works in the Pinacoteca Tosio Martinengo are all from Foppa's late period, around 1514–1515: the *Madonna and Child with Saints Faustinus and Jovita*, from the church of San Faustino in Riposo, with an interior that looks like a "prism of light"; the *Banner* from the parish church of Orzinuovi, in which the saints are ennobled by their austere simplicity; and the *Saints John the Baptist and Apollonius*, two fragments of a larger composition, in a landscape that is almost the main subject.

Late fourteenth-century painting in Brescia was also influenced by the work of foreign artists, from Flanders and Burgundy, and of major figures from other parts of Italy, such as Bramante and Leonardo.

Vincenzo Civerchio (ca. 1470–1544), born in Crema but active in Brescia as a young man, introduced such influences to the city: his polyptych with *St Nicholas of Tolentino, St Roch and St Sebastian*, dated 1495 and originally in the church of San Barnaba, combines his Foppa-inspired style with a variety of Lombard elements, particularly Leonardesque in the landscape and the figure of St Sebastian.

Floriano Ferramola (ca. 1478–1528) painted numerous frescoes on sacred and profane subjects in the city between Foppa and the next generation of Brescian painters. An incomplete cycle of frescoes originally in the Palazzo Calini in Vicolo Borgondio is a good example of his work. It was heavily influenced by the narrative style popular among painters from Cremona and Emilia. The scenes in this cycle are narrated in a flowing style, full of realistic details and attention to costume. Four of these frescoes are being shown in the Portland Art Museum exhibition and are illustrated in this catalog.

Although Brescia never entirely abandoned its Lombard origins, during the fifteenth century it was ruled by Venice and also absorbed its cultural influences. The pictorial innovations made by artists like Giovanni Bellini, Giorgione, Titian and Palma Vecchio at the end of the fifteenth century and the early sixteenth were followed with interest.

They conveyed the natural details and overall mood with a style that was later called "tonal" art, in which chromatic areas were created by varying the intensity of color and light, rather than by drawing and chiaroscuro. The influence of Venetian painting was fundamental to the three most famous sixteenth-century artists in Brescia: Savoldo, Romanino and Moretto, whose works make up the most important part of the collection.

Gerolamo Savoldo (ca. 1480/85–after 1548) is represented in the exhibition by his *Portrait of a Young Man with a Flute*, from ca. 1525. Its chiaroscuro and subtlety of light and atmosphere show the artist's links to Lorenzo Lotto. The Pinacoteca also has a *Nativity* (1540) by Savoldo: here the event is depicted in a very subdued manner, but is transfigured by the bright, lunar lighting of the night scene. The influence of Giorgione's night scenes is obvious, but Savoldo interpreted these with greater attention to detail. This interpretation of reality in its natural and human aspects derives from the innovative art of Foppa with Venetian and Lombard influences, along with those of Flemish artists. The same was true of Gerolamo Romani, called Romanino, and Alessandro Bonvicino, called Moretto.

The Pinacoteca has several paintings by these two artists. Private devotional paintings, huge altarpieces and detached frescoes all clearly illustrate the Renaissance in Brescia in which the tonal art of Venice was blended with the more subdued colors of Lombardy.

These common features, along with experiments in natural lighting, a total absence of rhetoric and a very lively form of realism did not give rise to a school of painting in Brescia, but they did unify the work of the different artists.

Girolamo Romani called Romanino (ca. 1484/87–1560) is represented in the exhibition by three paintings of exceptional interest and quality: the intense *Portrait of a Gentleman*, of ca. 1519; a tondo showing *Christ Carrying the Cross*, from the artist's maturity, where the Venetian tonalism of Giorgione and Titian merges with Savoldo's lighting innovations; and the *Lamentation over the Dead Christ*, set against a landscape that seems to amplify the dramatic devotional concentration of the scene.

One of the most characteristic Romanino works in the Pinacoteca is the altarpiece of the *Nativity*, originally in the church of San Giuseppe. Painted in the mid-1520s, it sums up the work of his early period: flowing brushstrokes, intensity of color

and a perspective composition that is halfway between architecture and landscape; all reminiscent of Venetian culture, particularly Titian. The formal smoothness, however, which goes beyond the austere rigidity of the Renaissance, is the result of Romanino's contact with Pordenone and Emilian artists. This altarpiece is one of the most success-ful examples of pre-Caravaggesque luminism: the Virgin's silvery-white cloak is gen-uine architecture of light, which enriches the intimate nature of the scene.

The *Supper at Emmaus* originally in the abbey of Rodengo is slightly later: it dates from the early 1530s. Alongside the bright, Venetian-style colors, the artist has given extraordinary attention to realistic details, even in their harshest aspects. This strong expressive tendency was also influenced by northern artists. It was already noticeable in the Cremona frescoes, but more evident after his work in Trento on the Buonconsiglio Castle. The exaggeration of the forms, which disrupts the formal neatness of his early works, is symptomatic of the religious unease and need for a moral renewal felt in Brescia in the first half of the sixteenth century.

The *Madonna and Child with St Nicholas of Bari and the Pupils of the Gramma-rian Rovelli*, dated 1539, from the dei Miracoli church is a fine work by Alessandro

Bonvicino called Moretto (ca. 1498–1554). Although influenced by the Venetian use of color, Moretto was closer to Lombard art and moderated this with a silvery-grey tonality reminiscent of Foppa. He avoided the provocative and controversial innovations of Romanino and was more noted for the sobriety of his paintings, as in this altarpiece, a solemn composition reminiscent of Titian. But Moretto was also able to give his paintings a familiar, everyday mood, expressed here in the affectionate gesture of the Child towards his Mother and the lively portraits of the children at the foot of the throne.

Moretto used solemnity and moderation to convey his austere religious sensibility, but occasionally reached peaks of expressionism that are not at all rhetorical, as in his late work, *Ecce Homo with an Angel*, originally in the Duomo Vecchio. The human and religious tragedies merge and are exalted by the choice of color, reduced practically to monochrome, and the bare simplicity of the composition.

The *Great Painters in Brescia from the Renaissance to the XVIII Century* exhibition allows about 15 years of Moretto's career to be followed in four paintings: two religious works (the *Annunciation* from ca. 1525–30 and the *Pentecost*, from ca. 1542–45) and two portraits from the second half of the 1530s (*Portrait of Tullia of Aragon as Salome* and the *Portrait of a Gentleman with Letter*).

The group of portraits by Brescian artists clearly shows their primary interest in portraying reality. This was also true of the Bergamo painter Giovanni Battista Moroni (ca. 1520–1579), who studied under Moretto. He was interested not only in the physical features of his subjects, but also the psychological aspect, as seen in his *Portrait of a Man of Letters (The Magistrate)*, dated 1560 and shown in this exhibition. Two small panels with the patron saints of Brescia, Faustinus and Jovita, can also be admired at the Portland Art Museum exhibition.

Lattanzio Gambara (1530–74), the fourth, great, Brescian Renaissance painter,

worked closely with Romanino and was also his son-in-law. He mainly painted fresco cycles, on both sacred and profane subjects, and was influenced by a variety of sources. He emphasized the need to break away from a purely Naturalist portrayal of reality and was the first to introduce Mannerist principles to Brescia. These elements can be seen in the two decorative frescoes in the exhibition, originally in a city *palazzo*. The powerful figures are connected by a compositional dynamism learned by the artist in Cremona, where he had trained in the workshop of the Campi brothers.

The four tempera paintings in the Pinacoteca by Antonio and Giulio Campi, active in the second half of the sixteenth century, are also examples of Brescian Mannerism. They show exemplary tales of justice from classical literature and the Scriptures, such as the story of *Susanna and the Elders*. The brothers' Mannerist style is evident in their attention to decorative detail, their interest in dramatic gesture and their quotations from classical antiquity.

Brescia came within the cultural sphere of Venice, but the Pinacoteca has only a few works by sixteenth- and early seventeenth-century Venetian artists.

The most important are the two paintings by Lorenzo Lotto (ca. 1480–1556/57). In particular the *Adoration of the Shepherds*, painted for a private client in 1530 during Lotto's second stay in Venice. The juxtaposition of strong color tonalities, the tense lighting structure and dynamic composition make it one of the most important works by this artist. He had early contacts with the art of northern European painters, and was later strongly influenced by Raphael.

The two most famous paintings in the Brescia collection are by Raphael (1483–1520), the great Renaissance painter from Urbino: an *Angel* and a *Christ Benedictory*. The *Angel*, purchased by Count Tosio in 1821, is a fragment of the *Coronation of St Nicholas of Tolentino*, painted by Raphael in 1501 at the age of sev-

enteen with another artist, Evangelista da Pian di Meleto, for the church of Sant'Agostino in Città di Castello. The painting was damaged in an earthquake in the late eighteenth century and the various pieces dispersed; the only other fragments that have been certainly identified are in the Louvre and the Naples Museum. The hand of Raphael is quite apparent in this *Angel*, where the young artist already revealed his composite background, with the influence of Perugino, Pinturicchio, Signorelli and possibly even Leonardo. This fragment is essential for gaining an understanding of the young artist's developments. He was already confident in creating a wide range of color harmonies and constructing a space distinguished by its soft lighting effects.

The small painting of the *Christ Benedictory* from about 1506 was probably a private devotional work. It also came from Count Tosio, who bought it in 1820 from a Pesaro merchant. The influence of Leonardo's painting and of classical sculpture is now more evident after cleaning, especially the way the figure is modeled in delicately "sfumato" sculptural planes. The painting has gained depth and the figure has a very spiritual mood; an almost unnatural light shines down from the sky, enveloping both figure and landscape. The latter has been pared down to its essentials, as was typical of Raphael's Umbrian and Florentine works.

The schools and trends of the seventeenth and eighteenth centuries are more difficult to examine as they are represented more sporadically, though again by important artists. There are two works by Luca Giordano (1634–1705), one of the most important artists of the Neapolitan school, whose work was influenced by the rudimentary naturalism of Jusepe de Ribera.

The most interesting figure in the Venice and Brescia area, also permeated by Lombard and Bolognese influences after the seventeenth century, was the Brescian Francesco Paglia (1635–1714). He is perhaps more renowned for having written a guide to the artistic heritage of the city. His *Adoration of the Shepherds* is from his full maturity, when his original classical training merged with echoes of Brescia's Renaissance tradition. The somber atmosphere enlivened by sudden patches of light and silvery reflections are quite typical of his art. Along with the chromatic influences of the Emilian painter Guercino, such aspects are also apparent in the four allegorical portraits recently attributed to him and shown in this exhibition.

Four paintings representing the four seasons through an anthropomorphic composition of fruit, flowers and vegetables in the manner of Arcimboldi, derive from the allegorical-decorative culture of Lombardy in the second half of the seventeenth century. These charming and vaguely disturbing works are attributed to Antonio Rasio, of whom little is known. His *Four Seasons* are shown here alongside two works by the Dutch artist Pieter Mulier (1637–1701), known in Italy as "Cavalier Tempesta" [Sir Storm], whose depth and luminosity of landscape certainly inspired Rasio.

Antonio Cifrondi (1657–1720) and Giacomo Ceruti called Pitocchetto (1698–1767) were important local eighteenth-century painters. They were referred to as "painters of reality" as they were primarily interested in depicting everyday events. Antonio Cifrondi's figures are set in compositions completely devoid of action, as in the *Seamstress* and the *Young Miller*, both in this exhibition, which are intended to exalt the humble daily toil of ordinary people. These paintings and the other two by Ceruti in the Pinacoteca (*Old Man Resting on a Stick* and *Old Woman with Stick*) were probably part of a single group painted for a Brescian residence.

The Pinacoteca Tosio Martinengo has some of the most important paintings by Giacomo Ceruti, from the so called "Padernello Cycle" (see the essay by Francesco Frangi). Three of these masterpieces are shown in this exhibition. They fully represent the human side of this artist, who was so removed from the Lombard-Veneto genre painting of the time. His painting technique also contributed to this, in scenes where the light color variations effectively convey his sympathy for the sorrowful condition of large sections of mankind.

Ceruti was not only interested in poor and derelict characters, called *pitocchi* in Italian, hence his nickname; he was also a highly respected portraitist, much sought after by the enlightened middle class and aristocracy. There are three of his portraits in the collection, documenting his psychological insight.

The genre of battle scenes is very well represented in the Pinacoteca. This kind of painting originally commemorated battles and wars, but soon became an independent art form depicting imaginary battles. Francesco Monti, called Brescianino delle Battaglie, was one of the most popular painters of this type of scene.

The works of the Brescian Faustino Bocchi, were among those classified as *bambocciata*. His paintings are of a funny and even irreverent nature: their message seems to be that art has a right to be "capricious" and imaginative, and even to satirize reality.

The great eighteenth-century Venetian school of view painters, of whom the most famous are undoubtedly Bellotto and Canaletto, is represented in the Pinacoteca by a small canvas showing an *Imaginary Architectural Composition* by Francesco Battaglioli, who was renowned for his carefully calculated perspective studies.

The Pinacoteca Tosio Martinengo collections are completed by the eighteenth-century schools with religious paintings and genre subjects.

Giacomo Ceruti in Brescia and the "Padernello Cycle"

Francesco Frangi

The Pinacoteca Tosio Martinengo's recent acquisition of four works from the "Padernello Cycle" by Giacomo Ceruti (the *Meeting in the Forest*, *Women Working*, the *Shoemakers* and the *Spinner*) could be seen as even more significant than the intrinsic qualities of the individual paintings themselves. Bringing these pictures to the public–and considerably expanding the gallery's existing representation of Ceruti works (the *Two Beggars* and the *Laundress*)–will help reawaken interest in this important aspect of eighteenth-century Lombard painting.

Ceruti created the series of genre scenes for the Avogadro family of Brescia during his youthful stay in the city, between the early 1720s and mid '30s. It was then rediscovered in the Salvadego family's Padernello castle at the end of the 1920s by Fausto Lechi, Alessandro Scrinzi and Giuseppe Delogu. Although it is to be hoped that the entire cycle may some day be reunited, including the dozen or so other works now in various private collections, this is an important step in that direction. In the meantime, these four examples offer the visitor a representative example of the whole ensemble.

Recognized as Ceruti's most important achievement, the cycle has constantly challenged scholars. Faced with that extraordinary world of beggars, cripples and war veterans; of humble craftsmen, young porters and girls busy learning women's work, they have asked about its meaning, and why the looming presence of those dirty, desperate figures should have been desirable in the exclusive, elegant rooms of a noble family's private gallery. Some critics have seen the paintings as an explicit social declaration and early sign of egalitarianism; others have suggested they reflect the newly awakened sense of charity among the ecclesiastical hierarchy and nobility that was common in the early eighteenth century.

Discussion on Ceruti's paintings has often avoided some aspects that are crucial to a correct interpretation of the Avogadro series. These regard the fact that the patrician clientele's liking for decorating their residences with cycles of paintings showing scenes of "low-life" was anything but rare in the late seventeenth and early eighteenth centuries. There were several examples in Lombardy alone. The collections of two Milanese aristocrats, Giovanni Antonio Parravicino and Antonio Vismara, assembled around the turn of the seventeenth century, had a conspicuous number of pictures of life-size tramps. They had been painted by the Danish artist Bernhard Keil known as Monsù Bernardo and the Austrian Giacomo Francesco Cipper, called Todeschini, both of whom played a leading role in popularizing such subjects in northern Italy. Considering

Giacomo Ceruti
*Woman Working at the Bolster
(Girls' School)*
private collection

that genre scenes made up complete, quite consistent cycles in some of the rooms in Parravicino and Vismara's country residences, it is clear that Ceruti's project followed an established precedent. Indeed, Ceruti's more dramatically pauperish subjects fitted quite comfortably into the rich repertoire of earlier genre painting. This is true of his painting *Women Working*, which includes the figure of a young girl learning to read in the midst of a group of women sewing, a device used repeatedly by Monsu Bernardo and by Todeschini to introduce the theme of education.

In addition to specifying the context of the commission and the iconographic tradition of the Avogadro paintings, these brief observations (for a wider discussion see Frangi, 1998, pp. 43–61) show how misleading it is to see them as faithful illustrations of the social reality of the time; almost as if snapshots of the typical social marginalization and ordinary life of Brescia in the early eighteenth century. Seeing the "Padernello Cycle" paintings in this way, and so attributing Ceruti with qualities that belong to the great French Realists of the mid-nineteenth century, means misapprehending the innovative and surprising nature of the works. This does not lie in the subjects they deal with and their presumed intention as "history pictures", to quote Francis Haskell. It is rather in the Milanese artist's ability to transform genre painting from within, not revolutionizing its patterns but radically altering its expressive register.

The solemn and serious mood of the Avogodro paintings, and all Ceruti's early works in Brescia including the *Two Beggars* and the *Laundress*, contrasts with the abundant production of popular subjects that preceded and accompanied them. Ceruti cast aside the light-heartedness of his contemporaries' approach to genre subjects, which they treated as comic, anecodotal, allegorical or purely decorative. The representation of the poor in these works is relegated to a more or less playful puppet theatre, in which the tramps, be they beggars or simple poor people, play the part of anonymous marionettes with stereotyped and "generic" faces. But something quite different happens in the Ceruti paintings. That puppet theatre is dispelled and, as if by magic, the figures stop being anonymous actors and suddenly go back to being real people; not apparently, but genuinely poor. As such, they are pervaded by a distressing awareness of their own destiny, easily read in the sad and weary face of the laundress bending before the fountain and the equally intense ones of the young seamstresses in the *Women Working*.

The humble actors of genre painting thus become austere, even grandiose presences, relegating the iconographic conventions that govern their appearance to simple pretext. The change of perspective is total, partly because the use of a language animated by the most profound realism gives it absolute credibility. It ensures that the figures are no longer presented as indistinct "types", but have the dignity of real individuals, dressed in real, dusty rags. Above all, their faces are studied with an objectivity and immediacy that can only be defined as portraiture. This is clearly echoed in the painter's contemporary work in that field, borne out by comparison between Ceruti's *Portrait of Giovanni Maria Fenaroli* of 1724 and his genre works. His great sensitivity and approach to each painting as a reaction before a real model reverberates in his genre scenes, inspiring him to endow each person in his humble stories with a specific character.

The "Padernello Cycle": clarifications on provenance and composition

The "Padernello Cycle" still presents numerous open questions. These relate not only to interpretation of Ceruti's style and culture, but also to the initial composition of the series, its original provenance and, consequently, its commissioning.

The cycle was rediscovered by Fausto Lechi and Alessandro Scrinzi (at the time director of the Brescia art gallery) at the end of the 1920s,[1] when it was already in the Salvadego's castle then extant in Padernello. It was presented for the first time as the subject of study in 1931 by Giuseppe Delogu, in what was the first systematic scholarly contribution on Ceruti (1931, pp. 195–210).

In trying to clarify reconstruction of the sequence of the cycle it is worth noting that Delogu's summary shows that there were then 13 Ceruti paintings of pauper themes in the Brescian castle, identified by him as follows (the numerical indications refer to the complete catalog of the painter by Mina Gregori, 1982): "*Man drawing wine*" (Gregori, 57), "*Hermit and devotee*" (ibid., 63), "*Boys playing cards*" (ibid., 58 or 66), "*Boys playing cards*" (ibid., 58 or 66), "*Beggar resting*" (ibid., 59), "*Woman working wicker*" (ibid., 60), "*Woman spinning and little beggar*" (ibid., 64); "*Urchins fighting*" (ibid., 62), "*Two beggars*" (ibid., 53), "*Dwarf*" (ibid., 50), "*Women Working*" (ibid., 51 or 55), "*Women Working*" (ibid., 51 or 55), "*Cobbler*" (ibid., 61).

In addition to these 13 works, Delogu noted the "*Basket bearer*" (ibid., 52;), also in the Salvadego's possession but at other premises, declaring its possible place in the same series. He also pointed out that other paintings by Ceruti, evidently similar to those he had noted, were at the time probably "retained by Countess M. Frigerio Salvadego".

Although Delogu posed no problems in identifying the provenance of the cycle, the catalog published in 1820 of the paintings in the Palazzo Fenaroli (now Bettoni), in Via Marsala, Brescia (*Galleria di quadri*, 1820, pp. 3–4) raised a first doubt. It suggested that eight of the paintings seen by the scholar at the Salvadego residence were in the Fenaroli city residence at the beginning of the nineteenth century, where the following works in particular were recorded, with reference to Ceruti:[2] "*Painting showing a girls' school*" (Gregori, 51 or 55), "*Two boys fighting, life-size*" (ibid., 62), "*Beggar resting on a rock, almost life-size*" (ibid., 59), "*Two youths; life-size seated fig-*

41

ures playing cards" (ibid., 58), "*Large painting, two paupers, man and woman in a wood, almost life-size*" (ibid., 63?), "*A dwarf in a town*" (ibid., 50), "*Woman spinning seated on a plinth, and with a life-size girl*" (ibid., 64), "*Two old people, man and woman, seated in the middle of the countryside; life-size figures*" (ibid., 53), to which the painting indicated as "*A beggar seated on a rock, almost life-size*" (ibid., 49) should probably be added.

The latter may be identified as the canvas formerly in the Seccamani collection in Brescia, and although not appearing among those mentioned by Delogu at Padernello, can probably be seen as an integral part of the original series,[3] given its similarity of style and composition to the other examples in the group (see Gregori, 1982, p. 432, no. 49).

This inventory correspondence[4] was incorporated into the exhibition catalog on *I pittori della realtà in Lombardia* (1953, p. 75) and for some time encouraged identification of the Fenaroli as the first owners of the series (this is the indication given, for example, by the 1953 catalog). But the studies conducted by Marini (1966, pp. 41–42; 1968, pp. 40–52), aimed at investigating the identity of Ceruti's commissioners, then managed to take a further step back into the history of the paintings. He was inspired by consultation of a late eighteenth-century inventory of the Avogadro family collection displayed in the *palazzo* "near San Bartolomeo" in Via Moretto, Brescia (now Bettoni Cazzago). In that document, almost certainly dating from between 1785 and 1800,[5] three genre works by Ceruti are indicated, in the reception rooms, as: "Painting above window of a woman spinning and a girl by the Milanese Ceruti", "Above window of a man and a woman, by Ceruti", "Above window by Ceruti".

The obvious similarity of the first painting described to the one showing the *Little Beggar Girl and Woman Spinning* (G. 64), reported as held by the Fenaroli in 1820 and the Salvadego at Padernello in 1931, and of the second painting to the *Two Beggars* (G. 53), also mentioned with the Fenaroli and Salvadego, convinced the scholar that the entire series was painted by Ceruti for the Avogadro family. This was supported by the observation that, with the extinction of the latter household in 1800, the entire Avogadro collection went by inheritance to the Fenaroli family,[6] which in this way also came into ownership of the Ceruti paintings in that collection at the beginning of the nineteenth century.

Ownership of the series was thus reconstructed as having begun with the Avogadro family, then moved to the Fenaroli at the beginning of the nineteenth century by inheritance, and finally to the Salvadego who, as again specified by Marini, came into possession of the works at an auction of the entire Fenaroli collection in 1882.[7] The odd increase in the number of paintings in the cycle remains, however, to be explained: from the three paintings cited in Avogadro ownership to the nine indicated with the Fenaroli and the 14 noted by Delogu. The notable increase from the Fenaroli to the Salvadego could be easily explained, according to the scholar, by the internal divisions of ownership within the Fenaroli family. On this basis it would be quite plausible for the paintings not shown in the 1820 catalog, but later found in Padernello, to have been held by some other member of the Brescian household

at the beginning of the nineteenth century, from which they then also went to the Salvadego by way of the 1882 auction.[8] The question relating to the Avogadro-Fenaroli transfer is, however, more complicated. The explanation offered for this by Marini involved subtle questions concerning the dating of the cycle itself, which the scholar claimed was entirely conceived after 1760. This is based on the fact that there is no mention at all of Ceruti's genre paintings in the Avogadro collection as listed in the guide to Brescia published that year by Carboni (1760, pp. 177–185). In this context, the indication of only three works in the subsequent manuscript inventory of the collection (which the scholar thought dated from only shortly after 1760) provided evidence, according to Marini, that the series was at that time still being painted and that other examples were added in the years following drafting of the manuscript.

These last considerations, however, were the weak link in Marini's argument. The reconsideration made some years later by Mina Gregori consequently focused on that crucial chronological question, in her still valid essay on the Milanese painter (Gregori, 1982, pp. 11–16, 41–49). Although accepting the reconstruction of the commission and subsequent ownership moves proposed by Marini, she rejected the possibility of such a late dating. She dated them rather to the painter's early years in Brescia (ca. 1720–ca.1734),[9] on the basis of aspects of style and culture, explaining their omission from the Carboni guide of 1760 as being simply due to a selective listing of the numerous works in the Avogadro collection.

Gregori conjectured that in addition to the works indicated by Delogu at Padernello, and to the *Basket Bearer*, also indicated by the latter as being owned by Savaldego, the series originally included other pieces. These were the *Seated Beggar*, recalled by Delogu in the Seccamani collection (to be identified, according to Gregori, as the "Beggar seated on a rock, almost life-size" mentioned in the Fenaroli catalog of 1820), the *Spinner* (G. 67) now on deposit at the Brescia Pinacoteca–which, Gregori also recalled, in support of its connection to the Avogadro group, had in previous decades belonged to a member of the Salvadego family–and possibly also the *Old Beggar and Bearer*: apart from the latter, these all seem to fit comfortably in with the other works.

There have since been other significant developments to these last stages of the story. These include in particular Maurizio Mondini's discovery of another invento-

ry of Avogadro possessions of 1734. This lists the family's paintings in the Rezzato
residence, in the environs of Brescia (Mondini, 1985, pp. 117–122). In light of the
above considerations, the earlier date of the document than the previous evidence
provides a clue to its importance. Indeed, three paintings appear among those listed. Despite the artist's name not being mentioned, all seem to qualify for recognition as additional pieces in the "Padernello Cycle". They are described as: "Two pictures of tramps above window with gilt frame" and "A picture of porters, above window", and were in the first and third reception rooms.[11] This part of the villa, sepa-
rate from the private apartments,[12] was used for entertainment and was where the
more prestigious works were hung. These included the two, full-length portraits by
Moretto and Moroni (respectively the *Nobleman* of 1526 and the so-called *Knight
with the wounded foot*) now in the National Gallery, London. They were at the time
hung to form a breathtaking pendant at the sides of the fireplace in the first reception room, the one with the two pictures of tramps by Ceruti.

Mention of the three paintings of tramps and porters in the 1734 document provides fairly significant confirmation of Gregori's chronological hypothesis. Although
the silence on the name of the painter would seem to leave margins for doubt, this
could be dispelled by the simple observation that those three works are none other
than the three paintings from the "Padernello Cycle" then also noted in the previously mentioned, late eighteenth-century inventory of the Avogadro's city *palazzo*.
Indeed, an overall analysis of the collection's history shows that many of the paintings indicated at Rezzato (including the two full-length portraits by Moroni and
Moretto) appear both in an inventory of the collection in the family's Brescian *palazzo*, drawn up in 1715,[13] and in the late eighteenth-century one. On this basis it may
by assumed that the 1734 document takes into account not only the permanent collection held in the country residence but also the temporary move to the city *palazzo* of many works normally kept in the former. Not by chance, the country residence
was subject to major alterations between the 1720s and '40s, which also involved
part of the collection being removed.[14]

If these suggestions are correct, the date of 1734 could give a certain earliest date
for at least three pieces in the Padernello series. These are the *Little Beggar Girl and
Woman Spinning*, the *Two Beggars*, and one of the two paintings showing porters that
make up the cycle. On the other hand, exclusion of Ceruti's genre works from the

Carboni guide of 1760 cannot be interpreted as a latest date. This is confirmed by a further very interesting item of information in our possession, which has so far escaped the attention of scholars engaged in this complicated but certainly not marginal question. It is provided by the notes of Charles-Nicolas Cochin's *voyage d'Italie* relating to that French traveler's stay in Brescia between 17 and 19 July 1751. He visited the Avogadro's city residence during his stay and gave an account in his diary of the main works in the collection. But then, after having recorded the paintings by the grand masters, mainly Italian, Cochin also noted other, less celebrated works that had impressed him. He also, fortunately, made a very eloquent description of these: "il y a en divers endroits de ce palais quelques tableaux de gueux & figures de modes, de grandeur naturelle, qui sont bien touchés, avec gout, de maniere assez grande, mais pas assez peints, plats & d'une couleur fort grise & foible".[15]

Although here, too, the name of the artist is missing, the indications relating to the subject, size and, above all, the pictorial and colorist aspects of those *tableaux* leave no doubt that they can be identified as the Ceruti masterpieces under discussion, whose presence *en divers endroit* of the Avogadro's Brescian residence can at this point already be ascertained in 1751. This is no small thing if read in the context of the historiographic debate of recent decades. Furthermore, the tone of the notes seems to suggest that Cochin saw and admired several more works than the three pieces recorded in the late eighteenth-century inventory. This may be because he was able to gain access to less prestigious rooms of the residence, allowing him to see other gueux (tramps) and other *figures de modes* (genre figures) by the Milanese painter.

It is precisely this "numerical" consideration that allows the last, delicate problem raised by the cycle to be dealt with: the strange increase in the number of its components noted in the move from the Avogadro to the Fenaroli and then to the Salvadego. The explanation for the Fenaroli-Salvadego transfer provided by Marini, and backed up by Gregori, seems quite convincing. But it is necessary at this point to make some further clarification regarding the increase between the Avogadro inventories and the Fenaroli catalog of 1820, justified by Marini in terms that, as seen, cannot be shared. Cochin's words provide a certain, and hardly negligible clue that the family's city residence may have contained a good many more paintings from the series than the three listed in the late eighteenth-century inventory.

Giacomo Ceruti, *Drawing Wine*
private collection

Giacomo Ceruti, *Woman Working Wicker*, private collection

Giacomo Ceruti, *Porter with Dog*
private collection

Furthermore, the 1820 Fenaroli catalog shows that the paintings mentioned largely coincide with those previously recorded with the Avogadro. This is such that any reading of the two lists gives the distinct impression that they are describing the same collection. Indeed, comparison of the inventories shows that the Fenaroli collection was largely formed with works acquired through inheritance in 1800 from the Brescian household that definitively died out in that year.[16]

It is therefore clear that the provenance suggested by Marini and Gregori for the Ceruti paintings may stand. At the time of the transfer by inheritance between the two families, it seems quite apparent that the Fenaroli's city *palazzo* was also furnished with works held in other Avogadro residences, probably in the country. This possibility inevitably leads to the conclusion already reached by Passamani (1987, p. 20) and more recently by Zani (1998, pp. 431–432), that the cycle that came to Padernello at the end of the nineteenth century was originally intended to decorate more than one of the Brescian noble family's residences.[17]

The above is what may be surmised on the basis of a perusal of the sources and documents. The substantial consistency of definition, style and expressive mood that seems to link the pieces of the cycle in the reconstruction made by Mina Gregori (with the exception mentioned) must also be noted. On this basis it is clear that, while some of these paintings may have been intended for some Avogadro residence other than the *palazzo* "near San Bartolomeo", this does not seem to exclude the possibility of seeing that memorable group as a substantially unitary undertaking and, for this reason, too, even more worthy of our admiration.

[1] Fausto Lechi and Alessandro Scrinzi's role in the discovery and appraisal of the cycle appears in particular in the words of Longhi (in *I pittori della realtà*, 1953, p. 65) and those of Antonio Morassi, who recalls being taken to Padernello by Scrinzi in about 1929–30 (Morassi, 1967, p. 364, no. 16).

[2] Ceruti's paintings are all recorded as being in the first room of the *palazzo*.

[3] The 1820 catalog also records a "laundress at the fountain, by Ceruti" at the Fenaroli home, almost certainly identifiable as the canvas of this subject in the Brescia art gallery, but not thought to be part of the series discussed here.

[4] An entry dating from shortly after the catalog, between 1821–25 (Gregori, 1982, p. 15), lists only three paintings in the first room of the *palazzo* from the series subsequently seen in Padernello, in addition to the *Laundress*, evidently indicating that the collection had been divided by inheritance in the meantime.

[5] The entire inventory is now published in Lechi, 1995, pp. 170–180.

[6] The transfer by inheritance between the two families occurred as a result of the marriage between the last heir Paola Avogadro, died 1800, and Bartolomeo Fenaroli.

[7] The catalog for the Fenaroli auction of 1882 has not yet been traced.

[8] The indications given in the entry of 1821–25 (see note 4) already documented the breakup of the collection following the family's internal hereditary divisions.

[9] Morassi had already intelligently posited an earlier dating of the cycle, on the basis of style relationships with the *Portrait of Giovanni Maria Fenaroli*, from 1724 (Morassi, 1967, p. 352).

[10] The addition of the painting from the Bettoni Cazzago collection is suggested by Gregori on the basis of the fact that the Bettoni counts bought the Palazzo Fenaroli at the 1882 auction, so it cannot be excluded that they also took possession of the Ceruti painting (Gregori, 1982, p. 16). Although this

supposition is quite viable, it must be said that of all the additions to the cycle suggested by the scholar, this in my opinion is the least convincing, partly because of the difference in size: the other examples in the series are all much smaller. As with the *Laundress* in the Tosio Martinengo art gallery, the possible presence of the work among the Fenaroli assets sold in 1882 does not necessarily infer its place in the series or provenance from the Avogadro. Regarding the pertinence of the *Spinner* to the series, see the entry for the painting in this catalog.

[11] The Rezzato inventory also mentions "a school with various figures" which inevitably suggests the "Girls' school" noted at the Fenaroli in 1820 and which may be indentified as one of the representations of girls at work in the "Padernello Cycle". It is, however, quite likely that the Rezzato canvas should be recognized as a work of the same subject by Peruzzini, already noted at the Avogadro home in 1715.

[12] The inventory specifies that the guest quarters were distinct from the personal apartments of Giovanni, Luigi and Achille Avogadro.

[13] It is published in Lechi, 1995, pp. 172–173.

[14] On the radical alterations made to the interior of the Palazzo Avogardo from at least 1722, see Lechi, 1974, pp. 102–119. Those works were commissioned by the brothers Girolamo, Giovanni and Luigi who, after the death of their father Scipione in 1715, altered the building in order to create three apartments for their respective families.

[15] The quote is taken from Michel, 1991, p. 418.

[16] The paucity of the Fenaroli collection prior to the arrival of the Avogadro works is also noted by Lechi, 1995, p. 171.

[17] There is at present no useful indication for identifying the member or members of the Avogadro families who had a role in commissioning the cycle, apart from the certainty that Ceruti was commissioned by the generation after that of Scipione Avogadro, who died in 1715 and had seven sons: Faustino (1675–?), Lelio (1677–1734), Giovanni (1682–1742), Achille (1684–1772), Gerolamo (1686–1763), Francesco (1687–1765) and Luigi (1690–1765). Whereas Marini and Gregori directed their attention toward Luigi, known also to have been the person to whom Maccarinelli dedicated his *Le Glorie di Brescia* (published 1747), useful observations relating to the cultural interests of other members of the family can be found in Passamani (1987, pp. 18–19).

Catalog

Brescian Painter

Frieze with Head of a Woman

1495–ca. 1500
Fresco: 37 1/2 x 118 1/8 in. (95 x 300 cm)
Inv. 1731

Provenance: Brescia, Palazzo Maggi al Fontanone, until 1973; Brescia, Pinacoteca Tosio Martinengo, since 1973; Brescia, Santa Giulia. Museo della città, since 1999.
Restorations: 1979, Scalvini & Casella, Brescia; 1999, Gian Maria Casella, Brescia.

The fresco was part of an imaginative, richly decorated frieze painted on the upper wall of one of the main rooms of the mansion owned by the Maggi, one of the oldest patrician families of Brescia. It was detached during partial demolition of the building and recovered along with 15 other fragments, which together covered about 50 meters of the room's perimeter (Stradiotti, 1979, pp. 149–154). The decorative cycle was found under a layer of plaster and so is severely damaged and has some extensive lacunae. It was connected to the big ceiling beams with carved corbels by a small wooden cornice; the remainder of which is without painted decorations (the ceiling had been whitewashed several times).

The frieze has two cornice moldings at the bottom, separated by a band with a decorative motif of leaves, stylized flowers and ampullae. The main upper band has a complex ornamental pattern in highlighted grey monochrome on a blue, red, violet, ochre and green background. Winged monsters, divinities, seahorses, monsters that are half men or women and half animals with leaf limbs, putti, big cornucopia, blossoming bouquets and lavish candelabra are all entangled in a recurring vegetal motif creating a fanciful whole. The original frieze comprised eight main monochrome motifs interspersed with 16 tondi. These circular imitation marble perspective frames contain half-bust color portraits. Five have been lost, leaving eight male and three female portraits. The highly personalized faces of all the subjects suggest they are portraits of the Maggi family.

The graceful female figures and spirited males in profile or full face are depicted with a dynamic, almost statuary

relief that makes them stand out from the blue background of softly lit sky. Careful attention to detail is evident in the individual clothing. The men wear the typical fifteenth-century cap, or "biretta", from which their long hair escapes in soft curls, while the women are modestly dressed in contemporary fashion. The best preserved female portrait is that of a young, blonde girl sporting the typical "coazzone": the big braid of hair falling down her back. This is carefully wrapped in a white veil, or "trinzale", and tied with a blue ribbon. A thin black string, or "lenza", surrounds her forehead and hair, which is divided into two smooth tresses from which two long curls escape. These fashions were typical of the last years of the fifteenth century and frequently recur in pictures of women from that period.

The solid definition, the sure modeling and the fluency of the painting date the portraits to the last years of the fifteenth century by a Lombard, probably Brescian, artist. Recalling the style of Bramante and influenced by Mantegna and Alberti, they represent the peak of Humanism in Brescia which had been assimilated here in the second half of the fifteenth century. This culminated in the return home of Vincenzo Foppa, who had been invited to teach painting and architecture, the start of work on the dei Miracoli church and plans to build the new Palazzo della Loggia. The painter of these portraits may have been close to the leadership of the Brescian school, given his pictorial expertise and perspective skill, though this is accompanied by a softer, more mild-mannered intonation and a marked propensity for decorative elements. An interesting comparison may be made with the some initials framing half-bust figures in the codex illuminated by Giovanni Pietro da Birago (formerly Duomo Vecchio, now Pinacoteca Tosio Martinengo, inv. 23), dating from the end of the fifteenth century and exhibiting "that grafting of Paduan-Ferrara and Lombard elements that had already been

seen in the second half of the fifteenth century in painting" (Panazza, 1964, p. 684).

The decorative friezes at the sides of the tondi confirm the training of the painter and his assistants in classical themes. They especially show a familiarity with Mantegna: the divinities and seahorses recall his engravings with these iconographic themes from the 1490s. The classical background and drafting suggest not only a direct knowledge of the originals but also of prints. These were a fundamental source of formal information at the time and ensured that ideas developed in central Italy were also brought north. The friezes also have a close resemblance to the work of Giovanni Antonio da Brescia, one of Brescia's leading engravers. He was in Rome in the first years of the sixteenth century and provided drawings for his home town. Engravings with friezes very similar to these ones, where human and animal figures turn into flowering branches, bouquets and other vegetal elements, have been cautiously attributed to him by Hind (1948, V. II, nos. 45–56). The same decorative motifs can be seen in the facade niche of the dei Miracoli church, confirming a common cultural denomi-nator in both painting and sculpture in Brescia at the time.

Other decorative cycles in fifteenth-century Brescian buildings have similarities to those in the Palazzo Maggi, from the figuratively complex examples painted by Giovan Pietro da Cemmo in a room in the San Barnaba monastery to the simpler ones found in various noble houses. In this case the artist has achieved an original decoration combin-ing his skill in the medium of fresco with his ability to real-istically portray the subjects and his elegance in ornamental design. The frieze could be by the prolific and skilled fresco and narrative painter, Floriano Ferramola (ca. 1478–1528), whose work is known from the first decade of the sixteenth century, but who was certainly active earlier. This is sup-ported by documentary evidence of a contact between Fer-ramola and the Maggi family, noted by Clemente Zillioli in the *Annali*, dated 1731, and extracts from the archives of the Maggi-Gambara family, joined by marriage into a single household at the end of the sixteenth century (Stradiotti, 1979, pp. 95–98).

Renata Stradiotti

Floriano Ferramola

(Brescia ca. 1478–1528)

Birth of Adonis
1510–12
Fresco: 65 1/8 x 65 in. (165.5 x 165 cm)
Inv. 35

The Falcon Hunt
1510–12
Fresco: 62 x 57 1/8 in. (157.5 x 145 cm)
Inv. 37

The Meeting of the Betrothed
1510–12
Fresco: 65 1/8 x 53 1/8 in. (166 x 135 cm)
Inv. 36

Two Servants and a Soldier
1510–12
Fresco: 42 1/8 x 22 3/8 in. (107 x 57 cm)
Inv. 39

Provenance: Brescia, Palazzo Calini, until 1845; Brescia, purchased by the Comune, 1903; Brescia, Pinacoteca Tosio Martinengo, from at least 1927 to 1999; Santa Giulia. Museo della città, since 1999.
Restorations: 1978–79, Romeo Seccamani, Brescia (inv. 39); 1986–87, Romeo Seccamani, Brescia (inv. 35, 36, 37).

The four frescoes were part of a big cycle decorating the main hall of the Palazzo Calini, Brescia, unique among sixteenth-century secular painting in the city. It is now divided between Brescia (Musei Civici d'Arte, Storia e Scienze), London (Victoria and Albert Museum) and Rome (private collection). The frescoes were detached and transferred onto canvas by Bernardo Gallizioli in 1845, as noted by Federico Odorici, when the *palazzo* was restored by the Vergine family (Odorici, 1853, p. 188; Mondini, Zani, 1986, p. 47).

Works carried out between 1985 and 1987 in the Palazzo Calini revealed various traces of old painting decoration on the walls of the main hall and an imitation scroll with the inscription [O]PVS / FLORIANI / FERAMOLA, confirming that the frescoes were painted by Floriano Ferramola, as widely corroborated by local historical sources.

Francesco Paglia described the frescoes in 1714 and advised looking particularly at the "beautiful hall, entirely painted with stories of Ovid, realistically expressed, early works by Floriano Ferramola" (Paglia, 1675–1714, ed. Boselli, 1967, pp. 158–159, p. 824).

Paolo Brognoli first referred to the painted scroll on a column with the painter's bold signature in 1826, and considered the work "the one that firmly establishes the merit of this distinguished painter, and I invite my fellow citizens and lovers of painting to admire it" (p. 299).

After the frescoes were detached, Ransonnet of Vienna condemned the removal of "those stupendous frescoes that were today brought down by those who have neither eyes to see nor heart to feel the sorrow of Brescian art" (1845, p. 27). In 1853 Odorici listed the subjects of the frescoes, now converted into "paintings" by Bernardo Gallizioli, while Paolo Fenaroli in 1877 described their various scenes. He paid particular attention to the *Carousel*, believing it marked the arrival in Brescia of the queen of Cyprus, Caterina Cornaro, in 1497, an event celebrated by the local press (Odorici, 1853, pp. 188–189, 200; Fenaroli, 1877, pp. 121–122).

The purchase of the *Carousel* in 1861 by London's South Kensington Museum, now the Victoria and Albert Museum, started a general reappraisal of Ferramola in the second half of the nineteenth century (Kauffmann, 1973, I, pp. 101–103). In those same years Giovanni Battista Cavalcaselle was making some identifications in the Brescia area in preparation for his *A History of Painting in North Italy*, but said simply that the decoration in the Palazzo Calini "is only represented by fragments" (Crowe, Cavalcaselle, 1871, ed. Borenius, 1912, p. 256). However, such fragments showed that Ferramola was evidently a painter "of character, who tends toward that fairly gracious manner as noted in the painters of Umbria", with references also to Ferrarese and Bolognese painters (Parisio, 1999, p. 73).

The desire to create a nucleus of works by Ferramola at the Pinacoteca Martinengo and to prevent further losses following the London sale of the *Carousel* prompted the Comune di Brescia to quickly decide, on 6 February 1903, to buy nine frescoes from the Palazzo Calini, ratifying its decision on 11 March. These were: *Birth of Adonis, The Meeting of the Betrothed, Soldier, Two Servants and a Soldier* and *The Falcon Hunt*, now in the Musei Civici di Brescia, and a *Falconer, Two Ladies*, a *Woman in Supplication* and a *Fight*, currently dispersed (Brescia, AMAS, inv. 35).

The recent publication of photographs from Stefano Bardini's historic archive in Florence provides some interesting information on this. They document not only the Ferramola frescoes now in the Brescian museums but three other pieces, recognizable as the *Falconer* (134 x 168 cm), *Two Ladies* (67 x 57 cm) and a *Woman in Supplication* (49 x 57 cm), which were previously shown in the 1903 Comune di Brescia list of purchases but mysteriously disappeared in the 1920s (Fahy, 2000, pp. 26–27, 92–95; Agosti 2003, p. 68, nota 70).

The five detached frescoes now in Brescia were exhibited in the *Galleria degli affreschi* of the refurbished Pinacoteca Tosio Martinengo from at least 1927, as recorded by Giorgio Nicodemi. He also noted others in private ownership, but not the other four bought by the Comune in 1903 (1927, pp. 24–25).

In 1974 Fausto Lechi published eight new detached frescoes, previously in the collection of Sir Humphrey Noble, bought on the London market in 1960 by a Rome collector: *Diana and Actaeon* (286 x 185 cm), *Nymphs in a Pond* (205 x 79 cm), *The Judgement of Midas* (285 x 185 cm), Greyhound (206 x 70 cm), *Maid with a Dish* (207 x 71 cm), *Pan* (205 x 79 cm), *The Sacrifice of Iphigenia* (285 x 186 cm) and *Apollo* (205 x 79 cm) (Lechi, 1974[1], II, pp. 181–193).

It is now therefore possible to graphically reconstruct the entire cycle, consisting of at least 17 frescoes, and to make an overall interpretation of their mythological subjects, following Elena Lucchesi Ragni (1995, pp. 107–111; 1991–93, pp. 23–43).

The walls were decorated with an elegant classical architectural frame, seen from the perspective of a central point on each wall, with arches resting on polychrome marble marquetry. Sturdy columns, pilasters and fluted pilaster strips provided an imaginary support for the ceiling beams. The architectural relationship between the real structure and the painted one was enhanced by decorative motifs on the monochrome frescoed base against a Pompeii-red background, with scenes taken from the triumphs of Petrarch framed with vegetal motifs. The pendentives featured monochrome tondi with archaeological-Mantegna inspired busts and scenes from the life of Muzio Scevola, one of the most representative figures of ancient Roman legend (Capella, 1997, pp. 91–100). A frieze above the arches was decorated with floral motifs, cornucopia and bouquets, with the Calini family crest at the apex of each arch. The latter was repeated on the wooden ceiling beams where the inscription MAR CHA can still be read, probably standing for Mariotto Calini, the commissioner of the work (Vaglia, 1987, pp. 145–146; Lucchesi Ragni, 1991–93, p. 24).

Seven of the ceiling brackets were also decorated with an unusual motif of musical notes accompanied by verses in Greek, Latin and Gothic. The entire decorative project may have been intended to commemorate its patron through painting, music and ancient languages. The musical score that is still legible seems to be a polyphony, possibly only for instruments as the words do not seem to rhythmically match the music. The individual Greek letters on one of the brackets are abbreviations of whole words, making it difficult to match words to music. The words are probably solely ornamental or celebratory. There are verses in Italian on another bracket, MADON[...] VOI [...] MA[...] SARA, possibly from a madrigal or court song or, more probably, from Ovid's *Metamorphosis*. Clearly the patron who commissioned these frescoes was familiar with classical literature since most of the scenes between the arches are based on Ovid Capella (1997, p. 99). Only the *Meeting of the Betrothed* and the *Carousel* have scenes from contemporary life with ladies and gentlemen sporting fashionable clothes, hairstyles and ornaments.

The Meeting of the Betrothed was on the south wall of the hall and seems to celebrate a meeting between a young gentleman and a lady, followed by a retinue of women. The latter are wearing the large, linear "camora" (dress) supported by the "faldia" (crinoline) with tight bust and low, square neckline; the dress of the central figure has conic sleeves "alla ducale", while those of the others are puffy and trimmed with vertical bands. The woman in the middle holds the plumed fan that was very popular from the start of the sixteenth century. The hairstyle with loose hair and "lenza", a ribbon with a gemstone or pearls falling from the centre of the forehead, was widespread at the end of the fifteenth century and the first years of the sixteenth. The man's clothing was also much in vogue in these years: the black surcoat with cut-away sleeves and fur edging gives an

overall sense of volume and three-dimensionality. This fresco was exhibited in the 1951 Turin exhibition *La moda in cinque secoli di pittura* precisely because of the interesting clothing worn by the figures, typical of north Italian fashion at the start of the sixteenth century (*La moda in...*, 1951, p. 28).

The southern wall was also decorated with the *Birth of Adonis*. Considerable attention has been given to the light effects and the ancient clothing of a hard, papery cloth in this entirely natural scene, derived from examples by Vincenzo Civerchio (Crema, ca. 1470–1544). The scene portrays the central moment of Ovid's story, when Adonis emerges from a tree by prizing open the bark, helped by Lucina the goddess of birth. On the left he is being fed and cared for by nymphs, who "place him on soft grass and bathe him with the tears of his mother. Even Envy should praise him for his beauty: his body is like that of the naked Cherubs painted in pictures" (Ovid Nasone, 1994, p. 411, canto X, 505–518).

The Falcon Hunt was on the south wall and probably told the story of the now mature Adonis and Venus, who "does not leave him, goes only with him. She who had always been accustomed to staying comfortably in the shade, to protect her beauty and increase it further, now goes through the hills and the woods, among the rocks and the thorny bushes, with her dress held above her knee like Diana, and sets the dogs on animals safe to hunt" (Ovidio Nasone, 1994, p. 413, canto X, 525–559). A falconer on horseback can be seen in a vast lake area, dressed in a style not seen in Italy later than Titian's frescoes of 1511 (Padua, Scuola del Santo); other men are occupied with everyday tasks. The background of an old medieval village is faithfully reproduced from the background landscape in Dürer's engraving *The Sea Monster* (1498–99). The rider in the middle distance and the young man in tights surrounded by dogs are also from engravings by Dürer, taken respectively from the *Galloping Horseman* (1495) and the *Five Horsemen and an Oriental on Horseback*. The animals and flowers in the foreground, also derived from Dürer, give the scene a courtly, fairy-tale atmosphere, with men in long, close-fitting tights joined to a "farsetto" (doublet) and with ribbons at their knee.

Ovid is again the inspiration for the fresco showing *Two Servants and a Soldier*, in which a woman treats the foot of another. This picture is completed by the detached

Soldier (Brescia, Musei Civici d'Arte, Storia e di Scienze, inv. 38) and the fragment with a woman and child still *in situ* on the south wall of the hall, referring to the events preceding the birth of Adonis. Myrrha had fallen desperately in love with her father Cinyras and, with the aid of her wet-nurse, had an incestuous relationship with him resulting in the birth of Adonis. On discovering the truth, Cinyras tried to kill his daughter. Here he is seen brandishing his sword, threatening Myrrha, who manages to escape, followed by Adonis, the child on the right, alluding to Myrrha's pregnancy. "Myrrha escaped under cover of night and, thanks to the darkness, managed to avoid death... She could hardly bear the weight of her legs. And then, not knowing what else to wish for, torn between the fear of death and the weariness of living, made this prayer... change me, denying me both life and death!... while she was speaking the earth mounded up around her legs, which became wood, her blood became sap, her arms branches, her skin hardened into bark" (Ovidio Nasone, 1994, pp. 401–411, canto X, 298–505). The classical influence of Bernardo Zenale is particularly evident in the architectural composition of this scene, with its effects of light, shade, perspective and the rhythmic scan of the spaces (Treviglio, Bergamo ca. 1450–Milan 1526). His style can also be seen in the hands and the big, slightly stumpy feet. The predominance of decorative friezes, cornucopia and candelabra to link the various episodes is also influenced by Zenale. Such motifs were to dominate the work of Ferramola, but Zenale was also to be highly renowned for them in Brescia (Averoldo, 1700, p. 99). The facial features of the man brandishing the sword and the one beside the women recall the work of the Bolognese painter, Amico Aspertini (ca. 1474–1552). This is particularly apparent if compared with the St George in the *Tirocinio altarpiece* painted in ca. 1504 by Aspertini, now in the Pinacoteca Comunale di Bologna (inv. 558).

Ferramola's frescoes were initially dated 1512 by Francesco Gambara (1820, pp. 249–250), more recently confirmed by Gaetano Panazza, who noted signs of the Emilian classical style of Lorenzo Costa (Ferrara, 1460–Mantua, 1535) and Francesco Francia (Bologna, ca. 1450–1517) (1963, pp. 996–997). A blend of Lombard and Veneto elements, however, convinced Roberto Longhi to date the entire cycle to 1518. He claimed these had been taken up by Ferramola after Romanino's return to the city

from Padua (Longhi, 1917, p. 114). The date of 1518 has also been supported by Mina Gregori (*Pittura del Cinquecento…*, 1986, p. 168), Francesco Frangi (1988, p. 712) and some more recent critics (Bizzotto Passamani, 1996, p. 435; Buganza, 1998, pp. 126, 130, 135–136).

But Ferramola's Palazzo Calini frescoes show a considerably more complex painting style than those of his signed and dated works from between 1513 and 1522: the *Virgin Enthroned with Saints Catherine and Albert of Jerusalem* in the Gemäldegalerie, Berlin (1513), the frescoed tondi with the twelve Apostles in the nave of the church of Santa Maria in Valvenda in Lovere (1514) and the canvas with the *Virgin and Child with John the Baptist and a Holy Father* in the Pinacoteca Tosio Martinengo (1522). The Berlin altarpiece and the Lovere frescoes exemplify the florid central phase of Ferramola's career, culminating in the painting of the grandiose *Annunciation* for the organ shutters in the Brescia cathedral between 1515 and 1518, now in Lovere. The Tosio Martinengo canvas, however, is from the painter's late career, marked by the resumption of his work in Santa Giulia (Santa Maria in Solario chapel and the Nuns Choir) and the frescoes for the chapel of Sante Croci in the Duomo Vecchio of Brescia in 1527, now completely lost (Zamboni, 1778, p. 110). Apart from the Berlin altarpiece, which shows the influence of the Cremona painter Francesco Casella (active in the first quarter of the sixteenth century) and close connections with the art of Zenale and Civerchio, Ferramola's subsequent works all have an evident simplicity. They are distinguished by an approach still based on the decorative works of the Brescian artists Vincenzo Foppa (ca. 1430–1515/16) and Giovan Pietro da Cemmo (documented between 1474 and 1532/33). Alongside the same recurring physiognomic, architectural and decorative motifs, they have a notably meditative, melancholy air and clearly late fifteenth-century style: elements that are quite absent from the Palazzo Calini frescoes. They are characterized rather by a mix of influences deriving both from the Lombard background of Zenale and Civerchio, and the Emilian style of Costa, Francia and Aspertini, with explicit citations from the northern art of Dürer.

So the frescoes are earlier in terms of style than the Berlin altarpiece of 1513, which marked a development toward more traditional stylistic components. It has none of the figurative elements Ferramola had assimilated between the end of the fifteenth century and the start of the sixteenth. Artists fully conversant with the new styles prevalent in Milan were in Brescia at this time: Civerchio, documented for the first time on 13 April 1491 in the home of Ludovico Martinengo and, especially, Zenale.

Further confirmation of a dating to between 1510 and 1512 for the Ferramola frescoes may be found in the clothing and hairstyles that were particularly in vogue between the last decade of the fifteenth century and the first few years of the sixteenth. The female figures in several scenes wear precious garments typical of these years and, especially, the "lenza" in their hair. This hairstyle can be seen in several works by Leonardo from his period in Milan, particularly the *Woman with Ermine* from ca. 1490, now in Cracow, and the *Belle Ferrannière* of 1490–95, now in Paris. The popularity of this fashion at the time is most evident, however, in Leonardo's presumed portrait drawing of *Isabella d'Este*, from ca. 1499, now in Paris, and the contemporary copy of it, now in Florence. The hairstyle and elegant profile in these are extremely similar to those of the ladies painted by Ferramola in the Palazzo Calini. The popularity of the "lenza" in those years, also in the Brescia area, is further confirmed by a fresco portraying a *Virgin Enthroned Nursing the Child* in the Pieve della Mitria a Nave (Brescia), dated 1501 at the top of the throne, in which the Virgin's hair falls loosely onto her shoulders and is tied with a ribbon around her head.

The costumes in Ferramola's frescoes also closely resemble examples from beyond the Lombard area, such as those in the scenes from the *Life of St Cecilia and her Husband Valerian*, painted between 1505 and 1507 in the oratory of Santa Cecilia, Bologna, for Giovanni II Bentivoglio by the Emilian painters Costa, Aspertini and Francia. This adds further strength to a proposed dating for the Brescian cycle to between the first and second decades of the sixteenth century.

Massimiliano Capella

Floriano Ferramola

(Brescia ca. 1478–1528)

Madonna Enthroned and Child with Saints Gregory and John the Baptist

1522
Oil on canvas; 74 x 76 3/4 in. (188 x 195 cm)
Inscriptions: on the scroll at the base of the throne: *OPVS FLORIANI FERAMOLAE. 1522*;
on the back of the throne: *AVE MARIA*
on the scroll held by Saint John the Baptist: *ECCE [AGNV]S DEI*
Inv. 1307

Provenance: London art market, 1964; Greenville South Caroli-na (USA), Bob Jones University, from 1964 to 1968; Brescia, Pinacoteca Tosio Martinengo from 1968.
Restorations: 1969, Ottemi della Rotta, Milan; 2005, Garattini & Malzani, Brescia.

The altarpiece is considered one of the major works of the painter Floriano Ferramola from Brescia. Ferramolo was a transitional figure in the city's art scene working in the period between the late sixteenth-century tradition of Vin-cenzo Foppa and Giovan Pietro da Cemmo and the innova-tion introduced in the seventeenth century by Girolamo Romanino, Alessandro Bonvicino, called Moretto, and sev-eral other foreign painters, most notably Vincent Civerchio from Crema. Among Ferramola's dated and signed paint-ings is the panel depicting the *Virgin Enthroned between Saint Catherine and Alberto Carmelitano* in the Gemäldega-lerie, Berlin (1513), the frescoed tondos depicting the *Twelve Apostles* in the central nave of the church of Santa Maria in Valvendra in Lovere (1514) and the canvas por-traying the *Madonna Enthroned and Child with Saints Gre-gory and John the Baptist* in the Pinacoteca Tosio Martinen-go (1522). These works are central in defining the artist's production.

While the Berlin altarpiece and the Lovere frescos doc-ument the mid-stage of Ferramola's career, which culminat-ed between 1515 and 1518 with the painting of the mag-nificent *Annunciation* for the organ panels of the Duomo in Brescia (now in Lovere), the canvas in the Pinacoteca Tosio Martinengo was painted in the final years of the artist's career. During this period the work in Santa Giulia recom-mensed (Santa Maria in Solario and the Nuns Choir) and in 1527 the artist executed the frescos in the Sante Croci chapel in the Duomo Vecchio in Brescia (Zamboni, 1778, p. 110), which have been completely lost.

While the other works by Ferramola have also been mentioned in the old guides to the city, little critical atten-tion has been paid to the Tosio Martinengo altarpiece, as it was only recently found and there is no information as yet about its original location.

Federico Zeri cites it among the many Italian works of art that came from American public collections, (Frederick-sen, Zeri, 1972, p. 69). In 1968, owing to Gaetano Panaz-za's zeal, the work was bought by the City of Brescia from the Bob Jones University in South Carolina (US) and was carefully restored in 1969, as shown by several archive doc-uments (AMAS). According to Gaetano Panazza and Camillo Boselli, the altarpiece is influenced by the school of Central Italy and, despite revealing a more formal style compared to Ferramola's early works, and repeats several components used by Foppa and the younger Romanino and Moretto (1974, pp. 46, 52, 53); the work is later cited by Francesco Frangi (1986, p. 167). By drawing on Rober-to Longhi's interpretation, which speculates that in the final part of his career Ferramola's art was influenced by Romani-no (1917, ed. 1956, p. 343), Bruno Passamani claims that the compositional structure of the work is based on the Berlin painting *Enthroned Virgin Between Saints Catherine and Albert Carmelitano* painted nine years earlier, and the enlarged forms are affected by Romanino's style (Passamani, 1988, p. 33). Stefania Buganza's more recent critical inter-pretation points out that the artist "conformed to a devo-tional and pietistic form of classicism, similar to that which permeates the work of Albertino Piazza da Lodi or Francia's final creative stage (1998, pp. 127, 128, 138).

The infrared reflectography of the altarpiece has revealed that the figures had been defined by the use of effective chiaroscuro and accurate drawing techniques in a way that is surprisingly close to the solutions already adopt-

Floriano Ferramola, *St John the Baptist in the Desert*
Brescia, Santa Giulia, Nuns Choir

ed by Foppa–to depict flesh tones and anatomy. The recent restoration has reduced the blur of the faces caused by a previous intervention; it would appear, therefore, that the classical inclination, often recorded by previous critics, has been replaced by a more accurate definition of the features.

The facial types, the architecture and the decorative motifs in the altarpiece are typical of Ferramola's style, and appear repeatedly in his late works. The features of the Virgin are identical to those already used for Mary in the panels depicting the *Annunciation* painted for the Brescia Duomo; the holy Pope could almost be superimposed on the *Apostle Simon* painted for the church of Santa Maria in Valvendra, in Lovere (1514); while *Saint John the Baptist* is exactly like the *Apostle Matthew* in Lovere (1514) and the figure of *Saint John in the Desert*, painted during the mid 1520s in the Nuns Choir (Capella, 1997, p. 90).

The composition of the scene, placed in an architectural space with a barrel vault, re-uses the traditional layout of the Holy Conversation theme, most probably recalling Perugino's *Virgin and Child between Saints James and Augustine* in

the church of Saint Augustine in Cremona (1494) and Vincenzo Foppa's later altarpiece of Mercanzia (1505–10).

It is the ample draperies that give the altarpiece its distinctive quality. The folds give movement to the robe of the Virgin and the cloak of Saint John the Baptist. A precious gold brocade in a pomegranate pattern, which appeared in Italy in the fourteenth century and would come to dominate its textile production in the fifteenth and sixteenth centuries, is reproduced in the cope worn by the Pope. It is trimmed with an embroidered border of saints, most likely the twelve apostles, in niches. The work in Tosio is the only altarpiece by Ferramola painted in the 1520s. It was painted at the time the artist was fully committed to his work in the Benedictine Monastery of San Salvatore and Santa Giulia where, with the help of his apprentices, he completed the frescos of Santa Maria in Solario (by 1524) and started the ambitious project of decorating the Nuns Choir (Capella, 2001).

A mood of contemplation and a trace of melancholy pervade the Santa Giulia cycles and Ferramola's other late works. The simplicity recalls the fifteenth-century teachings of Vicenzo Foppa and the celebrated decorative works of Giovan Pietro Da Cemmo. Although it is dated 1522, Ferramola's altarpiece belongs to this earlier tradition.

The work has been slightly cropped on all four sides and shows previous signs of distress. The restoration carried out in 1969 eliminated the varnish and the overpainting, while the recent restoration has recovered the intense contrasts and the lighting applied by Ferramola to differentiate the density of the damask cope and the lightness of the pope's robe with its silken reflections, the sheen of the velvet fabric draped on the back of the Virgin's throne and the softness of Saint John the Baptist's hide garment.

Massimiliano Capella

Giovanni Gerolamo Savoldo

(Brescia ca. 1480/85–? after 1548)

Portrait of a Young Man with a Flute

ca. 1525
Oil on canvas; 29 1/4 x 39 1/2 in. (74.3 x 100.3 cm)
Inscription on music score at top left:
Joanes Jeronimus sauoldis de / brisia / faciebat
Inv. 1765

Provenance: Sevenoaks (Kent), William Archer collection, prior to 1894, until 1924; London, Agnew Gallery, from 1924 to 1935; Florence, Alessandro Contini Bonacossi collection, from 1935 to after 1967; New York, Galleria Wildenstein, after 1967 and until 1975; New York, Peter Jay Sharp collection, from 1975 to 1994; Brescia, Pinacoteca Tosio Martinengo, since 1994 (deposit of the Banca Popolare di Brescia).
Restoration: ca. 1983.

The painting is in good condition overall. Small but widespread supplementary restorations have been made, particularly on the green tablecloth and the man's forehead, as shown by infrared examination in 1990.

Nothing is known of the painting prior to its appearance in an exhibition of early Italian paintings at the Royal Academy of London in 1894 (*Exhibition of works*, no. 117). At the time it was owned by William Archer, third duke of Amherst (1836–1910), in Sevenoaks (Kent). It was bought by the Agnew Gallery in London in 1924, then by the Alessandro Contini Bonacossi collection, Florence, in 1935. The Wildenstein Gallery of New York bought the painting after 1967, then Peter Jay Sharp, also of New York, purchased it in 1975. It was finally bought at auction in 1994 (Sotheby's, New York, 13 January 1994, lot 63) by the Banca Popolare di Brescia, which deposited it at the Pinacoteca Tosio Martinengo.

Presented at the 1894 London exhibition with an attribution to Giorgione, the painting was at that time recognized as a Savoldo work by Ffoulkes (1894, p. 268), who read the fairly obvious signature written on the music score.

Apart from some unexpected questions posed by Longhi (1927, ed. 1967, p. 151), the signature and the work itself have never been in doubt. Von Hadeln (1925, pp. 78–81) was the first to publish a reproduction of it in a scholarly context. Since then the painting has been widely acclaimed as one of the emblematic works of Savoldo's career. In the vast amount of literature on the painting, Ortolani (1925, pp. 172–173) and Venturi (1928[2], pp. 768–771) noted its chiaroscuro qualities and subtleties of light and atmosphere. Their words have been reiterated in subsequent commentaries, which also point out how these aspects presage the work of Caravaggio (Nicco Fasola, 1940, pp. 76–77; Christiansen, 1985, pp. 79–81). Ortolani's comments (1925) are useful for clarifying some of the painting's cultural references. His emphasis of the marked similarities to Lorenzo Lotto's work (particularly the *Portrait of Andrea Odoni*, of 1527) have been sustained by later scholars (see, for example, Pallucchini, 1944, p. XLII; Boschetto, 1963, no. 41; Ballarin, 1966). These have been more recently confirmed by Christiansen (1985) and especially Ballarin (1990), who compared the painting to two masterpieces of Lotto's portraiture from the 1520s: the *Young Man* in the Castello Sforzesco, Milan, and the *Dominican Monk* in the Museo Civico of Treviso from 1526. In his broader reconsideration of the painter's entire body of work, Ballarin convincingly dated the work to 1525, overturning Gilbert's earlier suggestion of 1539 (1985, p. 25), based on the wholly imaginary date (as Christiansen had already noted, 1987, pp. 80–81) he discerned in the book resting on the table.

Rosa Barezzani (1985, pp. 116–119) made some interesting musicological observations on the painting, identifying the instrument as a soprano recorder and noting that it is correctly held by the musician. She also claimed that the music on the hanging sheet of paper and in the book are two parts of the same composition for several voices, which begins with the words in the book she deciphered as "Regina Sanctissima". Gentili (1990, pp. 68–69) then suggested that the painter's signature on the music score means that

that part was to be played by Savoldo himself; the portrait would therefore be of a musician friend of the artist. Gentili also noted that a person playing a recorder is an anomaly in early sixteenth-century Venetian portraiture, where the more ennobling string instruments were preferred. Many recent studies of the painting have surprisingly ignored the important musicological discoveries of Colin Slim (1985, pp. 398–406). He identified the music on the hanging sheet and in the book as an early madrigal composition for four voices by the Paduan clergyman Francesco Patavino, or Francesco Santacroce (1487–ca.1556). It certainly dates from before 1524 and was conceived as the background to an anonymous sonnet, beginning "O Morte? – Holà!". The first 45 breves of the tenor part appear on the hanging sheet, while the more fragmentary parts of the *cantus* and *altus* (only the *bassus* is missing) can be read on the two pages of the open book. These are accompanied by some scarcely legible words, but Slim in any case rejects Rosa Barezzani's reading of these as "Regina Sanctissima".

The other iconographic elements in the painting are the small wall recess at top right containing two closed books and an inkpot, and the young man's elegant, round, feathered hat and fur-lined cloak. His clothing matches that of the donor, presumably a member of the Venetian nobility, in Savoldo's *Adoration of the Child* in Hampton Court.

Along with the latter, the *Adoration of the Child with St Francis and St Jerome* in the Galleria Sabauda and a cluster of other works including the dreamy *Young Man* in the Galleria Borghese, the painting documents an extremely successful stage of Savoldo's career in the mid-1520s when he was living in Venice. This period is distinguished by the altarpiece painted between 1524 and 1525 for the church of San Domenico in Pesaro, now in the Pinacoteca di Bera.

His work from that time has striking similarities to the contemporary works of Lorenzo Lotto, whom he certainly met during Lotto's stay in Bergamo. They then developed closer ties when the latter returned to Venice at the end of 1525.

The similarity with Lotto's portraits in the Castello Sforzesco and the Treviso museum give ample confirmation of the painting's cultural and chronological context. But further clues to the time and circumstances of its painting may be provided by identification of the composer of the music. The well-documented biography of the Paduan musician Santacroce (see Princivalli, 2001, pp. 307–374) shows that he was choirmaster at Treviso cathedral between 1520 and 1528. Savoldo was also in Treviso in 1521, having been commissioned to complete the unfinished altarpiece by Fra Marco Pensaben in the church of San Nicolò. It is therefore tempting to think that a relationship may have been established between the painter and musician at that time. Indeed, the certain dating of the musical piece to before 1524 and a plausible date of 1521 for a meeting between Santacroce and Savoldo help confirm that the portrait was painted shortly after. Identification of the anonymous earlier sonnet for which Santacroce composed this piece, and which appears in all the manuscripts and printed copies of the score, shows an enduring link between the poetic text and the music. Preserved in largely corrupt form, especially the two final triplets, the sonnet (see Torrefranca, 1939, pp. 166–174; Luisi, 1979, pp. 15–17) is written as a dialogue. It revolves around the request of the poet, tormented by Love, to be visited by Death. But she tells him she is unable to take hold of his heart, as Love holds it jealously. Surely this gloomy conversation is the reason for the melancholy of the subject of this masterpiece.

Francesco Frangi

Girolamo Romani called Romanino

(Brescia 1484/87–1560)

Portrait of a Gentleman

ca. 1519
Oil on panel; 19 7/8 x 16 5/8 in. (50.5 x 42.3 cm)
Inv. 82

Provenance: Brescia, Paolo Tosio collection, from at least 1815; Comune di Brescia, by bequest of Paolo Tosio, 1844; Brescia, Pinacoteca Comunale Tosio, from 1851 to 1906; Brescia, Pinacoteca Tosio Martinengo, since 1906.
Restoration: 1912, Fratelli Steffanoni, Bergamo.

The panel was noted as a portrait in the "style of Titian" in Paolo Tosio's collection as early as 1815. Alessandro Sala described it as a work by Titian (1834, p. 123) and again, in 1844, as a "Portrait with striped surcoat, by Titian" (*Riepilogo*, 1844, no. 20). The painting is mentioned in the topographical list of the Tosio collection as being "in the second east room" (*Oggetti d'arte*, 1846, no. 38).

There is no known archive information documenting the portrait's changes of ownership before it came into Paolo Tosio's possession. Paolo Guerrini and Gaetano Panazza thought it could be identified as the portrait of an unknown person, by Titian according to some and by Lorenzo Lotto according to others, registered in 1820 with number 439 in the Paolo Brognoli collection in Brescia (Guerrini, 1927, p. 243, no. 439; Panazza, 1965, p. 59). But this is not easy to sustain as the painting was already in the Tosio collection in 1815. Furthermore, in a handwritten note, Camillo Boselli identified the *Portrait of Ludovico Ariosto* by a Veneto Master of the sixteenth century, in the same bequest from Paolo Tosio (inv. 111), as portrait 439 in the Brognoli collection (Brescia, AMAS, inv. 82).

Romanino's small panel was still recorded as a work by Titian in the Pinacoteca Tosio catalog written by Federico Odorici (1853, p. 152). Ten years later, Odorici was the first to attribute the portrait to Romanino (1863, p. 10, no. 64). This was then confirmed by Tommaso Castellini in the Pinacoteca catalog, where the work was described as "Romanino self portrait" (1868, p. 37, no. 171). This attri-

bution may have been inspired by discussions between Odorici, Castellini and the "connoisseurs" who at that time visited Brescia. They included Otto Mündler, a purchasing agent for the National Gallery of London, who was in Brescia between 1855 and 1858, and Giovan Battista Cavalcaselle, who made identifications in the Brescia area between 1865 and 1869 in preparation for publication of the *History of Painting in North Italy* (London, 1871). Crowe and Cavalcaselle, who first attributed the panel to Girolamo Romanino with critical justification, saw in the portrait a "bust likeness of a gaunt bearded man […] which gives a high opinion of his powers" and noted repainting on the forehead and hair (1871, ed. Borenius, 1912, p. 284).

The attribution to Romanino was then accepted by subsequent critics: Ariassi (1875, p. 9), Morelli (1890, p. 290), Jacobsen (1896, p. 29) and Berenson (1907, p. 283). Dates from 1518 to 1530 were suggested for the work in the twentieth century: Giorgio Nicodemi dated it to around 1520–25 in 1925 (pp. 95, 196), while Adolfo Venturi suggested a date of around 1520 (1928², pp. 823, 855). This was based on its similarity to the Cremona frescoes and the anxiousness that accompanies the psychological pathos of the figure. The similarity of the clothing worn by Romanino's *Nobleman* and that of the *Portrait of a Young Man with Book* by Lorenzo Lotto in the Castello Sforzesco museums in Milan prompted Anna Maria Brizio to date the panel to around 1530 (*La moda*, 1951, p. 35). Panazza (1958, p. 117) and Maria Luisa Ferrari (1961, p. 330) then placed the portrait among Romanino's early works and proposed a date of around 1519–20, shifted to 1521 by Gilbert (1959, pp. 261, 263–264).

On the occasion of the big Girolamo Romanino exhibition at the Duomo Vecchio in Brescia in 1965, Gaetano Panazza wrote of this portrait that "the dating to ca. 1519 is

the most probable" (p. 59). Bruno Passamani also attributed it to the young Romanino, again from about 1519, in the guide to the Pinacoteca Tosio Martinengo (1988, p. 53). Alessandro Nova confirmed this in his monograph on the painter, suggesting "the first months of 1520" and pointed out that "compared to the Buckingham Palace *Nobleman*, who is still shown in almost frontal pose, in the Tosio portrait there is a first attempt to place the subject in a three-dimensional space" (1994, p. 236).

The panel was shown in Turin in 1951 at the exhibition entitled *La moda in cinque secoli di pittura* precisely because of the interesting clothing of a military flavor worn by the man: a jerkin, probably of black satin, set off by a jacket with pink-orange horizontal stripes and a white shirt emerging from the collar. This fashion was typical of the years between the second and third decades of the sixteenth century. The hat that originally adorned his head, read with greater clarity in the x-ray, has the same "biretta" shape as those worn by other men painted by Romanino between 1519 and 1520 (*Christ before Caiaphas*, the man facing the lady, *Crowning with Thorns*, the armed man in the left foreground, Cremona, Duomo, 1519; *Marriage of the Virgin*, the man on the left behind St Joseph, Brescia, church of San Giovanni Evangelista, ca. 1519; *Portrait of a Gentleman*, Budapest, Szépmüvészeti Múzeum, ca. 1520).

The intense, melancholy nobleman is lit by a ray of warm, oblique light that gradually and gently draws the figure out from the impenetrable darkness of the background. The pink-orange of the jacket emerges powerfully from this, recalling the Venetian tonalism of Giorgione and Titian. The depth and languor of the subject's gaze were well described by Panazza, who saw an anticipation of the imminent "move from the Renaissance to an age of serious contrasts, of acute spiritual crises" (Panazza, 1965, p. 59).

The close similarity of the figure of the nobleman to some heads in the Cremona frescoes (1519) and the painting of the *Marriage of the Virgin* in the church of San Giovanni Evangelista (ca. 1520) confirm a date for this portrait of around 1519.

The state of conservation is not good; Cavalcaselle mentioned repainting on the forehead and hair (Crowe, Cavalcaselle, 1871, ed. Borenius, 1912, p. 395), while Boselli noted that the x-rays made in the early 1970s, though not showing any change in the background, confirmed the presence of a hat (Panazza, Boselli, 1974, p. 79). This has since been confirmed by more recent x-ray studies (2004).

Massimiliano Capella

Girolamo Romani called Romanino

(Brescia 1484/87–1560)

Christ Carrying the Cross

ca. 1545
Oil on canvas; DIAM. 33 7/8 in. (86 cm);
with the frame 37 x 36 5/8 in. (94 x 93 cm)
Inv. 83

Provenance: Cancelleria (archives) of the Ospedale Maggiore, Brescia; Pinacoteca Tosio, Brescia from 1864 to 1888; Pinacoteca Tosio Martinengo, Brescia from 1888 to 1906; Pinacoteca Tosio Martinengo Brescia, from 1906.
Restorations: 1914, Fratelli Porta, Milan; 1955, Ottemi della Rotta, Milan; 2005, Garattini & Malzani, Brescia.

The original location of *Christ Carrying the Cross* of the Pinacoteca Tosio Martinengo and its pendant, a tondo depicting the *Virgin with Child* now hanging in the Sala del Consiglio (council hall) of the City Hospital in Brescia is unknown. However Francesco Paglia, the first source available, (1675–1714) describes the works as being in the archives of the Ospedale Maggiore of San Luca before 1714 and attributes them to Girolamo Romanino (ed. Boselli, 1967, p. 419).

In Paglia's apograph *ueriniano* manuscript, probably one of the last written in the monumental work *Giardino della Pittura*, the author notes the two paintings in the Cancelleria dell'Ospedale: "two tondos appear to be set in the wall, one portraying the Virgin of Heavens who is gazing adoringly at the sleeping Baby Jesus [...]. In the other the Saviour is depicted carrying the Cross. His colour is so vivid and so dignified that he seems to be one of Giorgione's best figures; his robe is depicted so well that it shows the fineness of silk and the accuracy of the handiwork. These two paintings are by the celebrated Gerolamo Romanino, among his best and most accurate works" ["vedonsi incastrati nel muro due rotondi, nell'uno de quali effiggiata s'ammira la Vergine del Cielo, che con dolce maniera adora il suo Bambin Gesù mentre dorme [...]. Nell'altro si finge dipinto il Salvatore che porta la Croce così al vivo espresso e con tanta fierezza colorito che sembra de migliori di Giorgione con veste intorno così ben fatta che par che mostri la finezza della

Seta, la sottigliezza del lavoro. Queste sono due tele della celebre mano di Gerolamo Romanino delle sue cose più studiate, e megliori."]

In the same manuscript Paglia praises the expressive quality of the depicted figures with several verses. Of *Christ Carrying the Cross* he writes: "which mortal man weighed down by his sins / could portray my Lord so vividly? / How is it that I can read on His lips / the dignity of His pain / manifested with tears / & a tender and pious manner / which should speak to us of Love / but that vivid color / of red rubies / that has been painted on His Divine lips / by the wonderful touch of Art / leaves us speechless" ["chi mai col sagro peso ove morio / così al vivo ritrasse il mio Signore? / Come mai in quel volto / leggo la maestà del suo dolore? / In lagrime disciolto / con atto dolce e pio / ci parleria da le sue labra Amore; / ma quel vivo colore / d'animati rubini / che su' labri divini / gli ha 'l mirabil pennel tinto, e spremuto / de l'Arte a lo stupor, rimase muto"] (Brescia, Biblioteca Queriniana, ms. A.IV.8, p. 313 and the slip of paper inserted in the binding between pp. 312 and 313).

Around the mid eighteenth century the work is described as being in the same location next to the *Virgin and Child*, and once again it is attributed to Romanino, this time by Francesco Maccarinelli and Giovanni Battista Carboni. (1747 and 1751, ed. Boselli, 1959, pp. 265, 266 and 1760, pp. 96–97). In the nineteenth century, the painting is mentioned by Alessandro Sala (1834, p. 79) and by Federico Odorici (1853, p. 88). On 16 December, 1857 during his stay in Brescia, Otto Mündler who was the purchasing agent for the National Gallery in London, described there being in the Archives of San Luca "Two round pictures by Rumanino [...] a Holy Virgin; indifferent, and a *Christ Carrying the Cross*, admirable, of noble character; perfect in form & in expression; diligently executed & light in tone." (*The Travel Diaries…*, 1985, p. 191). Therefore Mündler had already pointed out the two distinctive characteristics that Romanino was able to confer to the small picture which have always been emphasized by critics: the formal balance in the composition and the skilful use of light.

In 1864, in order to safeguard its preservation, the painting of *Christ Carrying the Cross* was "temporarily handed to the Pinacoteca Civica Tosio", along with the large painting by Moretto depicting the *Supper at Emmaus* (inv. 88) and in 1882 the City of Brescia exercised its pre-emptive right to buy the works belonging to the Amministrazione degli Ospedali Civili di Brescia (civil hospital administration); however payment was made only in 1911 (AMAS).

The painting was listed for first time in the *Elenco dei Quadri Antichi appartenenti alla Galleria Comunale*; the list was forwarded to the Ministry of Education on 18 November 1864 (ASB, ASC, rubrica XIV, affari diversi, 1/5a). It was cited by Tommaso Castellini, along with other paintings from the Ospedale Maggiore (1868, p. 47) and by Giovan Battista Cavalcaselle, who was carrying out some research in the Brescian area, between 1865 and 1869 for the monumental publication *A History of Painting in North Italy* (Crowe, Cavalcaselle, 1871, ed. Borenius, 1912, pp. 278, 279). Cavalcaselle's notes, which accompanied his drawing made from the painting, state: "Bright silvery hues […] Warm flesh tones and silvery shadows […] Executed with readiness and fluency / His paintbrush flows easily" ["Tinta luminosa argentina […] Carni con lumi caldi ed ombre argentine […] Eseguito con molta facilità e prontezza / Il pennello scorre facile".] (Parisio, 1999, plate VII, pp. 113, 114 and 202) Cavalcaselle himself was the first to liken *Christ Carrying the Cross* to a series of related paintings by Romanino composed of the *Nativity* in the Pinacoteca Tosio Martinengo (inv. 84), the *Mystic Marriage of Saint Catherine* in Memphis (inv. 61.202) and *Our Lady of Assumption* in Sant'Alessandro church, Bergamo; he also was the first to suggest it was painted prior to 1534. In 1875 and 1879 Giuseppe Ariassi and Federico Odorici recalled the painting again in the Pinacoteca Tosio (Ariassi, 1875, c. 11; Odorici, 1879, p. 17, no. 19) while in 1888, following the opening of the new Pinacoteca Comunale Martinengo, the tondo by

Romanino was transferred to the new museum and placed next to the *Nativity*, to which Cavalcaselle had already likened it stylistically (*Brescia. Pinacoteca Tosio…*, 1888, p. 3, no. 23). On that occasion Gustavo Frizzoni commented that in the two works brought together, there was "a particular approach to the use of color […] a brightness of tone, especially in the clothing pattern" ["uno speciale problema di colorito […] una lucentezza di tono, massime nei motivi dei panni"] (1889, p. 28).

When the Pinacoteca Tosio Martinengo opened, Romanino's *Christ Carrying the Cross* was placed in a room dedicated to the Brescian Masters, and in 1939 it was shown in the exhibition *La pittura Bresciana del Rinascimento*. The catalog described the work as "expressing pain", and maintained that Romanino's passion "lends silver reflections and precious silken radiance to Christ's white robe" (p. 267).

According to Gaetano Panazza, the "well invented" tondo is of Venetian colors, light and tone; however he points out that the "most Venetian of our painters of the sixteenth century, comes from the westernmost Venetian mainland, next to the Lombardia region, owing to the plastic consistency of his forms and the silk sheen of the garments" (1968, p. 122).

While the attribution of the work to Girolamo Romanino has never been questioned, the date of its execution suggested by the critics has wavered between 1525 (Jacobsen, 1896, p. 30) and 1545 (Ballarin, 1993, p. 448).

Proceeding from the date attributed by Emil Jacobsen, Adolfo Venturi saw in the painting "sharp shadows and harsh light" and placed it among the works executed by Romanino after 1525 (1928[1], pp. 841, 855), as is confirmed by Rossana Bossaglia (1963, p. 1052).

Nicodemi associated the tondo to the *Christ Carrying the Cross*, now in the Brera and to the San Domenico altarpiece in the Pinacoteca Tosio Martinengo (inv. 96) and estimated the date of execution between 1530 and 1532 (1925, pp. 144, 196, 223, n. 3). Maria Luisa Ferrari also dated it around 1530, and in 1965 the painting was shown in the *Girolamo Romanino* exhibition bearing the same date (Ferrari, 1961, plate 61; Panazza, 1965, pp. 83, 84). In a review of the exhibition the Tosio Martinengo painting was once again likened to the one in the Brera by Florence Kossoff who maintained that: "the Milan version of *Christ Carrying the Cross* still appears to this reviewer as

Girolamo Romani called Romanino, *Christ Carrying the Cross*
photograph taken during the restoration in 1955

a crude interpretation of the painting in the Tosio-Martinengo Gallery" (1965, p. 518).

The research carried out by Alessandro Ballarin on sixteenth-century Brescian painting, provided a new critical interpretation of the Girolamo Romanino catalog, and the paintings that Cavalcaselle associated with *Christ Carrying the Cross* were chronologically shifted from the beginning of the 1530s to the 1540s, while the tondo of the Pinacoteca Tosio Martinengo was dated around 1545 (1993, pp. 443–449). There followed yet another dating of 1545–46, put forward by Alessandro Nova (1994, p. 326).

If the painting is dated to around the mid 1540s, then it was produced at a time when Romanino had a renewed interest in the compositional and stylistic elements that were close to the lagoon painting tradition of Giorgione and Titian, which he had previously experienced earlier in life, and become interested in Giovanni Gerolamo Savoldo's rendition of highlight effects. Indeed, the work of this phase is characterized by a much richer palette, where lighting is used to heighten the silkiness of draperies and clothing, as can be seen in the cloaks of the *Nativity* in Brescia or the *Mystic Marriage of Saint Catherine* in Memphis, and in Christ's radiant sleeve in the Pinacoteca Tosio Martinengo tondo.

The painting is in a gold rectangular frame made in 1914 by Giuseppe Faccin from Vicenza and is in good condition (AMAS). During the restoration carried out by Ottemi della Rotta in 1995, pigment was transferred from the old canvas to the new one because of the poor adhesion of the primer; on that occasion some pentimenti were revealed, especially in the hands, showing that originally Romanino had conceived the scene with two figures, Christ in the center and a thief on his left, whose hands and profile emerge in the layer underneath, at the top and on the bottom left of the work. The well known iconography of *Christ Carrying the Cross*, attributed to Giorgione and Titian in the School of San Rocco in Venice, was therefore re-used by the Brescian painter, who had already employed it in a painting of the same theme now in the Brera, previously in the Averoldi collection in Brescia. The former is perhaps related to *Christ Carrying the Cross with a Thief* by Romanino no. 434 in the collection of Paolo Brognoli (Guerrini, 1927, p. 243). Upon executing the final Tosio Martinengo version of the tondo, Romanino chose a more intimate, more dramatic rendition, marked by the mystic isolation of the figure of Christ, according to the older iconography of *Christ Carrying the Cross* made popular by Giovanni Bellini. This allowed Romanino to create a scene of great perspective virtuosity by placing the figure of Christ in a foreshortened Bramante-like oculus, according to Panazza (1965, p. 83), and to make use of a series of "variations on the theme of the circle" (Nova, 1994, p. 326), which are clearly seen in the juxtaposition of the circular monochrome band, which gives the illusion of depth to the oculus, with the thin halo placed between the curved lines of the landscape in the background and the circle created by the arms of Christ. Hence Romanino conveys his genius on the small canvas, with an extremely dynamic composition where the use of the straight lines of the heavy Cross breaks the dominating circular composition and allows the figure of Christ to leap into the foreground with surprising drama and a strong plastic quality.

The restoration carried out in 2005 revealed that Romanino had painted over the hands of the thief in the visible area of the painting but left them in the area covered by the frame. This detail, together with the greenish colored oil-based primer used in the preparation of the canvas, seems to confirm that the painting was originally conceived in its current dimensions and circular shape.

In the sacristy of the Sant'Alessandro church there is a replica of *Christ Carrying the Cross* painted by Luigi Lombardi (1858–1940) (Prestini, 1986, p. 40); it was most likely intended to replace Romanino's painting in its original setting once removed. Therefore it can be assumed that Lombardi's work was moved to the church of Sant'Alessandro along with other furniture, because of the changes affecting the San Luca hospital starting from the mid nineteenth century, as the hospital belongs to its parish.

Massimiliano Capella

Girolamo Romani and workshop

(Brescia ca. 1478–1528)

Pietà with St Paul, St Joseph and Devoted Women

second quarter 16th century
Oil on canvas; 94 1/8 x 66 in. (239 x 167.5 cm)
Inv. 94

Provenance: Brescia, San Giuseppe, until 1869; Brescia, Pinacoteca Tosio Martinengo, since 1869.
Restorations: 1962, G. Battista Simoni, Brescia; 1989, O. Nonfarmale, Bologna.

The painting shows the Virgin with the Dead Christ in her lap and four saints. On the right is St Joseph, recognizable by the staff he is holding, and a saint normally identified as Mary Magdalene. However, the royal crown visible at her feet suggests the latter is more conceivably St Catherine of Alexandria. On the left is St Paul with a sword and book, and a second saint without attributes who is a more plausible candidate for the Magdalen because of her proximity to Christ's feet. The three crosses of Calvary and the towers of a fortified city stand out in the background of the vast twilit landscape.

The painting has fairly obvious problems of conservation, due partly to the damage caused by an early, imprudent cleaning mentioned by Averoldo (1700, p. 39). He noted that it had been "washed" and covered with "too much varnish" shortly before publication of his book and, as a consequence, had lost some of its splendor. The altarpiece was then "restored" a few years later by the Casale painter Ferdinando Del Cairo (Maccarinelli, 1747 and 1751, ed. Boselli, 1959, p. 121), possibly because of the earlier work. The latter operation cannot be confused with the washing noted by Averoldo, as Del Cairo (1665–1743) did not move to Brescia until 1701.

The altarpiece was restored in 1989, revealing a general deterioration of the paint film, particularly in the Virgin's dark cloak and St Joseph's yellow one, which have lost much of their original form. The figure of Christ has suffered similar damage. The impairment of the painting layer on the presumed St Catherine has exposed a fairly obvious pentimento in the position of her head, which was originally further back. X-rays made in 1989 showed that other alterations had been made to the latter figure during painting, including the removal of a string of pearls adorning her hair.

The painting was originally in the Franciscan church of San Giuseppe in Brescia, where it was the altarpiece of the second chapel on the left dedicated to St Mary of the Passion. Archive studies made by Prestini (1989, pp. 76, 82, n. 39) show that the chapel was built by Giovan Pietro Cazzago, who not only left a considerable sum of money to the convent but also instructed his heirs to spend 50 ducats on an altarpiece and carry out other decorative works to the chapel. Unfortunately the documents do not show the date of Cazzago's will, which would obviously provide a certain *terminus post quem* for dating the painting. The chapel was also decorated with frescoes, now lost, which the earliest guides all attribute to Romanino (Faino, 1630–69; ed. Boselli, 1961, p. 94; Paglia, 1675–1714, ed. 1967, pp. 101, 789) and were probably commissioned by Cazzago's heirs.

The painting was considered the work of Romanino up until the first half of the twentieth century, since when it has been the subject of a fairly lively debate. Although Romanino is confirmed as having conceived the work, various doubts have been expressed about its actual painting. The problem was raised by Ferrari (1961, pp. 35–36; tavv. 57–58), who identified Romanino's work only in the figure of Christ and the section of landscape, and suggested that the other five figures were by Callisto Piazza. Her opinion was more or less shared by Rossana Bossaglia (1963, pp. 1047, 1051) and Sciolla (1971, p. 22), who also extended Piazza's work to the landscape. The painting was then presented in the catalog for the 1965 Romanino exhibition in Brescia as a work painted by him and some anonymous assistants (Panazza, 1965, pp. 108–109). More recent stud-

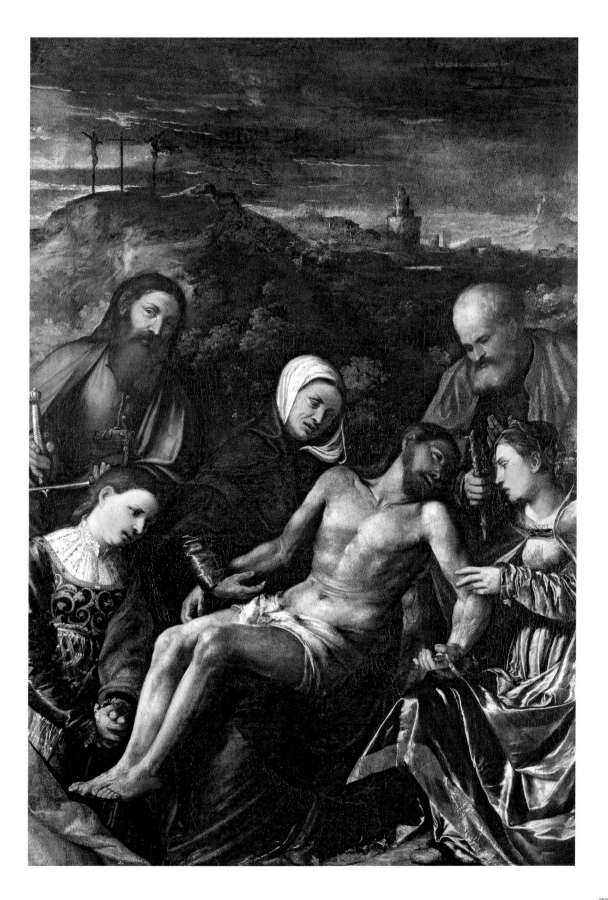

ies by Renata Stradiotti (1989, p. 194), based partly on the 1989 restoration, have suggested excluding Piazza entirely. Alessandro Nova (1994, pp. 331–332) confirmed it as being entirely by Romanino in his *catalogue raisonné* of the Brescian artist's work, emphasizing the high quality of some details, such as the cloak of the presumed St Catherine of Alexandria, though also considering it "a tired work".

Similarly contrasting opinions have been expressed on its dating. Those who claimed a contribution by Callisto Piazza have inevitably dated the painting to slightly before 1530, which marked the end of this Lodi artist's stay in Brescia. A date of around 1540 was suggested by Gaetano Panazza (1965, pp. 108–109), while Alessandro Ballarin (1993, p. 397) and Nova (1994, p. 332) have opted for between 1545 and ca. 1548.

The positioning of the body of the Dead Christ in the Virgin's lap is based on the German Vesperbild iconography. The extremely linear symmetrical composition harks back to late fifteenth-century and early sixteenth-century models. This contrast with the painting technique where the palette and impasto combined with a masterly lack of inhibition clearly relate to Titian. The section of landscape with its evocative flares and atmospheric sensitivity also recalls Titian. The style of Romanino is most apparent in precisely these latter elements, though the types of figures are also largely in keeping with his repertoire. Furthermore, the articulate pose of Christ almost exactly resembles that of the figure in the *Pietà with St Paul, St Joseph and Devoted Women* in the parish church of Ospitaletto Bresciano, a work generally agreed to be by this artist and for which a fairly late date of around the mid–1540s (Nova, 1994, p. 319, no. 91) has recently been suggested.

So although the work is undoubtedly similar to Romanino's mature style, inconsistent passages cannot be ignored.

Not all of this work seems to be of the same quality as the known works by the artist. Compared with the impressive detail of the presumed St Catherine of Alexandria and her magnificently highlighted clothing with its expert iridescence, the painting of other sections of the work is less striking. The lack of expressiveness in the head of St Joseph hardly matches the psychological insight that usually distinguishes Romanino's figures; while the dress of the presumed Magdalen on the left is painted in a conscientious, slightly mechanical way that contrasts not only with Romanino's usual technique but also with the greater fluency of brushwork in the saint in front of her.

Although the condition of the painting advises against making a precise, systematic distinction between its varying levels of quality, there is no doubt that it is only partly by Romanino. He must have been assisted in its painting, certainly not by Callisto Piazza (whose style is not consistent with that of the painting), but by one of the numerous assistants and apprentices who were active in Romanino's workshop, particularly from the 1530s. The most assiduous of these was Daniele Mori, who certainly collaborated on Romanino's frescoes in Val Canonica in that same decade. But archive documents also mention many other assistants (Boselli, 1977, II, pp. 272–274), suggesting not only how this painting was produced, but also other works painted entirely or partly by his assistants, such as the processional standard of the church of Saints Faustino e Giovita Maggiore in Brescia (Nova, 1994, pp. 321–322, no. 95).

The similarities to the layout of the *Lamentation* in Ospitaletto Bresciano suggest dating the work to the mid 1540s, as proposed in recent literature.

Francesco Frangi

Alessandro Bonvicino called Moretto da Brescia

(Brescia ca. 1498–1554)

Annunciation

1525–ca. 1530
Oil on panel; 16 1/2 x 22 3/4 in. (42 x 58 cm)
Inv. 87

Provenance: Brescia, Paolo Tosio collection, from at least 1832; Comune di Brescia, by bequest of Paolo Tosio, 1844; Brescia, Pinacoteca Comunale Tosio, 1851; Brescia, Pinacoteca Tosio Martinengo, since 1906.
Restorations: 1932, A. Sala, Brescia; 1955, Ottemi Della Rotta, Milan; 1988, Scalvini, Brescia.

The small panel depicting the *Annunciation* has a very spiritual mood, evident in the gestures and expressions of the Virgin and the archangel. The clarity of color in the clothing, from vivid yellows and reds to bright blues and greens, softens in the shadow between the two figures. This merges into the flesh tones, then pales into infinite tones of light in the landscape beyond the window. The dove of the Holy Spirit appears from a thick cloud that overlaps the heads of the angel and the Virgin and which Gaetano Panazza (1958, p. 122) thought rather "heavy".

Although the painting has always been described as being in good condition since the time of Crowe and Cavalcaselle (1871, p. 415), it has been restored three times: in 1932 (Sala), 1955 (Ottemi Della Rotta) and in 1988 (Scalvini) for the Moretto exhibition in Brescia. The old parquetry was replaced in the latter, but "a chromatic material cleaned in the past and extremely patchy in some sections" was also revealed (Brescia, AMAS). Reflectographic studies show the angel was first drawn further back, with differences in the clothing and arms more widely spread, possibly to give a greater sense of depth (Stradiotti, in *Alessandro Bonvicino…*, 1988, pp. 214–215), but moved forward at the painting stage to involve the worshipper.

This intense spiritual involvement is better appreciated by comparing the panel to its model: an engraving by Marcantonio Raimondi (Terraroli, in *Alessandro Bonvicino…*, 1988, p. 283), which Moretto also used to make a preparatory drawing, now in the Accademia Carrara (inv. 550), for the damaged *Annunciation* frescoed over the door of the church of San Cristo in Brescia (Lucchesi Ragni, 1980, pp. 95–98; *Alessandro Bonvicino…*, 1988, pp. 231–232). Moretto moves apart the two figures taken from Raimondi to introduce a structure in the style of the architect Bramante that opens onto the landscape. But the Virgin already has her left arm and the book she was contemplating in front of her, altering her gesture of wonder toward the worshipping angel. This perception increases in the small panel and the disquieting announcement becomes a silent dialogue, imbued with devotion and spiritual sharing.

Everything helps arouse such sentiments: from the Leonardo influences, mediated through Savoldo, seen in the thin golden hair of the angel, the light-softened flesh, the greens of nature and the shaded blues of the mountains, to those of Titian in the tonal sections and the Raphaelesque composition.

The date of the painting has been shifted from the 1520s to the 1530s, but I think it ought to be moved back to where Longhi had placed it (1929, p. 111), along with other "simple 'presentations' like those of Foppa": the *St John the Baptist* in the Venice Accademia, the *St Francis* in the Pinacoteca di Brera in Milan, the *St Ursula* in the Castello Sforzesco in Milan, the *Christ Resurrected and his Mother* in the Pinacoteca Tosio Martinengo, the Orzinuovi altarpiece and the *Madonna* previously in the Frizzoni collection.

A merging of Milanese classicism with that of Titian and Raphael took place at this time, identified by Alessandro Ballarin as being around 1527 (*Le siècle de*

Titien, 1993, p. 425), after the *Assumption* in the Duomo Vecchio in Brescia. This is also apparent in the altarpiece of Sant'Eufemia (Brescia, Pinacoteca Tosio Martinengo, inv. 90), the *Coronation of the Virgin and Saints* (Brescia, church of SS. Nazaro e Celso) and the *St Justina with Donor* (Vienna), all of which have expressive features similar to those of the *Annunciation.*

The popularity of the painting is confirmed by several copies or replicas of the same size: a panel in oil in the Hague state museums, a canvas sold by Christie's in 1915 and another auctioned by Agnew and Sons of London in 1926 (Begni Redona, 1988, pp. 549–560).

Marco Rossi

Alessandro Bonvicino called Moretto da Brescia

(Brescia ca. 1498–1554)

Portrait of Tullia of Aragon as Salome

ca. 1537
Oil on panel; 22 x 15 3/8 in. (56 x 39 cm)
Inv. 81

Provenance: Brescia, unknown location, before 1814; Milan, Teodoro Lechi collection, until 20 July 1814; Milan, Giuseppe Longhi collection, from 20 July 1814; Brescia, Paolo Tosio collection, after 1831; Comune di Brescia, by bequest of Paolo Tosio, 1844; Brescia, Pinacoteca Comunale Tosio, from 1851 to 1906; Brescia, Pinacoteca Tosio Martinengo, since 1906.
Restoration: 1986, Gian Maria Casella, Brescia.

The subject is a young, richly dressed woman holding a sceptre in her left hand. Her forearm rests on a block of marble with an inscription referring to Salome, the dancer responsible for the beheading of John the Baptist. The sceptre is classically decorated with acanthus leaves and the branches of a laurel bush can be seen on the dark background. The subject has been variously identified as Herodias, Tullia of Aragon and Salome, but is now known as *Tullia of Aragon as Salome*.

No purchase documents for the painting were found in the Tosio family archive, though its provenance from a nunnery (Biagi, 1886, p. 656) seems unlikely.

It was mentioned in a list of Teodoro Lechi's paintings as *Herodias in fur holding a rod*, bought in Brescia (Lechi, 1968, p. 204) and attributed to Moretto. It was then the object of an exchange on 20 July 1814 between Lechi and Giuseppe Longhi, the Brera engraver and renowned author of reproduction prints (Morandotti, 1996). Tosio probably acquired it shortly after Longhi's death (1831) when his large collection of art was sold (Beretta, 1837, p. 69).

An engraving was made when the painting was in Longhi's collection by his student Caterina Piotti, a Milanese printmaker. This was presented at the Milan Accademia's 1823 competition as a "half figure taken from a painting by Moretto" (*Atti*, 1823; Giuseppe Longhi, 1999, pp. 127–129) entitled *Herodias* (*Esposizione*, 1823; Gianfranceschi, Lucchesi Ragni, 1997). But Piotti had removed the reference to the beheading of the Baptist. This must have been evident in the painting, however, as shown by its original identification as Herodias. It was then printed by Giovanni Raffaelli with a dedication to the collector Giovanni Battista Sommariva. In this version the figure is for the first time identified as *Tullia of Aragon*, a sixteenth-century poet. Two couplets under the title, possibly suggested by Longhi (who liked to add commentaries to his engravings), show which iconographic elements were used for this identification: "What my origin was / the golden sceptre shows; / What my talent is / the laurel crescent shows". ["Qual fu la culla mia / Mostra lo scettro d'oro; / L'ingegno mio qual sia / Mostra il crescente alloro."]

There has been no reason to refute this interpretation. The allusions to Tullia's poetic skills, symbolised by the laurel, to her high culture and her presumed royal origins are clear. She was born in Rome (1505/10–1556) to a courtesan mother; her father was reputed to be Cardinal Louis of Aragon, the nephew of Ferdinand I of Naples.

The fame of the poet-courtesan, whose life so typified the Renaissance and its contradictions, spread in the eighteenth and early nineteenth centuries through reprints of her work (for biographical details on Aragona see Celani, 1891 and Rosati, 1936).

The panel was listed as *Tullia of Aragon*, numbered 2, in the *Riepilogo* of Tosio paintings (1844), as it was in the subsequent topographical inventory (*Oggetti d'arte*, 1846), where it was numbered 46 and located in the second east room of the Palazzo Tosio. It again appeared as *Tullia* in the first guide to the Pinacoteca Tosio's prints (Odorici, 1854, p. 8).

Although attribution to Moretto has never been in doubt since publication of the Lechi list, recognition of the subject varied between Tullia, Herodias and Salome in the second half of the nineteenth century due to the ambiguity of the iconography. In 1888 Federico Odorici suggested it

QVAE SACR IOANIS
CAPVT SALTANDO
OBTINVIT

Caterina Piotti, *Tullia of Aragon. Poet of the XVI century*
by Alessandro Bonvicino called Moretto da Brescia,
dated 1823, engraving, private collection

could represent a historic figure "dressed up" (p. 21, no. 39: "Tullia of Aragon dressed as Herodias").

Bernard Berenson interpreted the figure rather as Salome, Herodias' daughter, whose erotic dance won her the Baptist's head from Herod, but gave the location of the painting, by an obvious oversight, as the episcopal palace (1907, p. 262).

The painting is reproduced in *The masterpieces*, 1909, as Salome; it is defined as "Salome, or portrait of Tullia of Aragon" in the exhibition catalog of *La pittura bresciana* (1939, p. 203).

But Salome's normal attributes, the act of dancing or the dish containing the saint's severed head, have been replaced by the royal sceptre and the laurels of poetic glory.

A link between the figure of Salome and a sixteenth-century poet of royal origins as suggested by the iconography may be found in a biographical detail: they both led a debauched or fairly disordered life due to their mothers' influence.

The corrupting influence of Herodias on her daughter Salome is noted in the Gospels, while Tullia of Aragon often expressed her shame and regret at the life of a "courtesan" thrust on her by her mother, and her ambition to redeem herself through culture, poetry and art in general. This is particularly evident in her *Rime* and her dialogue *Della infinità d'amore* (Venice, 1547), inspired by the enthusiasm for Petrarch and neo-Platonism in mid sixteenth-century Italy. Although little more than well-mannered scholastic exercises, these works show her aspiration to compensate for the less noble side of her life with literature, and the influence of the scholars she associated with in various cities (Bernardo Tasso and Sperone Speroni, along with Girolamo Muzio, Benedetto Varchi and Francesco Molza). The conviction that Tullia's reprehensible condition was due to fate and that she was consequently tormented by an unsatisfied desire to become more virtuous is also evident in other compositions dedicated to her. Molmenti (1898, p. 107) wrote that "Bonvicino painted […]Tullia of Aragon, who at a still young and early age regretted her past misdeeds".

Moretto's portrait may represent Tullia's wish to create an image of herself in the social role she aspired to. This is evident in the rich but modest, dignified clothing, and the signs of nobility and the arts. The portrait may have been commissioned by a member of the Venetian circle she frequented, if not by Tullia herself, and was possibly painted during her stay in Venice between 1534 and 1537. The stylistic elements match those of other works by Moretto from the same period, but the "dressed up" subject, hairstyle and clothing may be likened to the more conventional *Portrait of a Woman as St Agnes* in a private collection (probably from the workshop; Begni Redona, 1988, p. 352).

The *Dialogo d'amore* by Sperone Speroni (1542) takes place between Tullia and Bernardo Tasso at the time of Tasso's departure from Venice (1535 or 1537). This marks the end of their relationship, and the poet-courtesan expresses her desire to change. Tullia also refers to the propriety of the "portrait" as a painting genre in the dialogue (the portraitist mentioned is, inevitably, Titian). By a charming coincidence, Moretto's portrait was painted in the same period the dialogue was composed and published.

Giovanni Battista Cavalcaselle saw the painting on one of his inspection visits to the Brescia area between 1865 and 1869, and made a pencil sketch of it (Parisio, 1999, p. 50). In Cavalcaselle's draft (Parisio, 1999, p. 146) the notes accompanying the "workshop panel" specify that the "flesh is much restored" […] in the "painting by Bonvicino of a noble genre that recalls some figures and the art of Lorenzo Lotto".

Crowe and Cavalcaselle (1871, ed. Borenius, 1912, p. 303) later described it as "a careful work, injured in the flesh parts by restoring, and reminiscent of Lotto". Da Ponte (1898, p. 48) also noted the damage from touching-up and excessive varnishing.

Gombosi (1943, pp. 48, 100) dated the portrait to 1540 or immediately after, which has been generally accepted (Begni Redona, 1988, pp. 354–356).

The painting is plausibly from between the second half of the 1530s and the early '40s, possibly ca. 1537. Moretto was seeking a different direction and trying to join a new intellectual and aristocratic circle in that period. He wanted a new career as a "courtly" portraitist to give his work greater breadth and prestige. The portrait is consistent with this stage of his life: in 1535 he briefly frequented the court of Isabella d'Este in Solarolo (Frati, 1898; Begni Redona, 1988), he painted a portrait of Aretino, mentioned in letters of 1543 and 1544 by the latter (though otherwise unknown), and worked on several large commissions in the Veneto area (Verona, Monselice).

Moretto partly idealised the poet's facial features, using forms seen in his other female figures, but her own physiognomy is apparent in the slightly pronounced nose, the light eyes and the line of the neck. Reflectographic studies showed a complete, precise drawing beneath, though without the main volumes, which had been left to be built up at the painting stage (Stradiotti, 1988, p. 217). The light from above left highlights the pearls in her hair, the rich velvet cloak and the soft folds of the fur. It defines the features of her face and casts a deep shadow onto the inscription in the foreground. The laurel leaves behind the figure, applied in thick paint with dense brushstrokes, suggest another "metaphorical" portrait: that of Giorgione's *Laura*.

Ida Gianfranceschi, Elena Lucchesi Ragni

Alessandro Bonvicino called Moretto da Brescia

(Brescia ca. 1498–1554)

Portrait of a Gentleman with Letter

ca. 1538
Oil on canvas: 45 x 39 3/8 in. (114.5 x 100 cm)
Inv. 151

Provenance: Brescia, Alessandro Sala collection, until 1846; Brescia, Alfonso and Caterina Sala, until 1853; Brescia, Pinacoteca Comunale Tosio, by bequest of Francesca Coradelli Catazzi and Caterina Coradelli Feroldi, at the wish of their cousin Caterina Sala, from 1853 to 1888; Brescia, Pinacoteca Comunale Martinengo, from 1888 to 1906; Brescia, Pinacoteca Tosio Martinengo, since 1906.
Restorations: 1955, Ottemi Della Rotta, Milano; 1988, Giuliano Scalvini, Brescia.

It was the wish of Caterina Sala that this portrait come to the Pinacoteca. In the nineteenth century it belonged to the painter, writer and collector, Alessandro Sala (1777–1846). It was then inherited, along with other paintings, first by his brother Alfonso, then his sister Caterina. The portrait and two other paintings were formally donated to the Pinacoteca Comunale Tosio in 1854 by the heirs and cousins of Caterina Sala, Caterina Coradelli Feroldi and Francesca Coradelli Catazzi; in 1948 it was decided that the donation, originally known as the "Sala bequest" should be named the "Sala-Feroldi bequest" (Brescia, AMAS).

Moretto's painting is mentioned as being in the Pinacoteca Comunale Tosio for the first time in 1853, in the "second room" (Odorici, p. 152). In the guide to the Pinacoteca, published in 1854 but probably written earlier, Federico Odorici noted that "the gallery will soon be enhanced by three paintings left by the noble widow Sala: one by Moretto" (p. 18). In 1863 the "Portrait, by Buonvicino called Moretto", numbered 169, was positioned in the alcove of the building (p. 16).

There is no archive information on ownership before the painting went to the Sala family. But a "Portrait with fur and black beret, by Moretto, of an unknown person" is recorded in the 1820 lists of the Paolo Brognoli collection in Brescia at number 408, which could be the work now in the Pinacoteca (Guerrini, 1927, p. 243).

The portrait is of an elegant gentleman dressed in a padded jacket of light red satin, with broad slits (crevé) similar to those in the military jacket known as a "coletto". The voluminous, very elegant over-garment is of black textured velvet, with turned-back collar; the typical trousers joined to stockings can also be seen. The splendor of the clothing, and especially the slits in the fabric, permitted in civilian clothing only to the wealthy classes, clearly suggest the subject is a nobleman. In addition to the sheet of paper in his right hand and the oil lamp on the shelf, other objects that had been later painted over were revealed by x-rays made at the time of the 1988 Brescia exhibition: there were books and, on the window sill, a ceremonial Roman helmet with plume. These would indicate a literary man, possibly a poet who wrote of military exploits, or an educated nobleman and skilled fighter (Stradiotti, 1988, pp. 213–214).

When it was donated to the Pinacoteca Tosio, the portrait was described as showing "an elder of the Sala family, by Moretto". Then, at the end of the nineteenth century, critics suggested identifying the gentleman as Pietro Aretino (Fleres, 1899, pp. 267, 285–286). But there is a truncated noble crest in red sealing wax on the back of the frame in which the shape of a prawn ["gambero"] can be made out. Gaetano Panazza interpreted this as the possible mark of a member of the Gambara family (1968, pp. 127, 227). The subject was a noble and educated man, a combatant, probably of about 35–40. Information available on the Gambara family members alive in the first half of the sixteenth century suggests that these characteristics describe Gianfrancesco Gambara, son of Maffeo. He was noted as being particularly skilled in music, poetry and arms. Two large volumes were dedicated to him by Mario Nizzoli in 1535: *Marii Nizolii Brixellensis Observationvm in M. T. Ciceronem prima pars et secunda pars*.

The first critical study of the portrait was made by Giovan Battista Cavalcaselle, who saw references to Titian and Sebastiano del Piombo, and noted abrasions in the flesh and the background (Crowe, Cavalcaselle, 1871, ed. Borenius, 1912, p. 300). Jacob Burckhardt, in some notes of 1862–63 on the *Por-

trait of a Young Man by Moretto in the National Gallery of London, published posthumously in 1898, related it to "a work by Moretto in the Brescia gallery that is not inferior to the one named. It is a portrait to the knee, larger than life size, of a nobleman in cherry-red jerkin, bright red hose, overgarment in black damask and beret. The person is seated at a table with a letter in his hand and on the right there is a glimpse of landscape" (Burckhardt, 1898, ed. 2001, p. 422, no. 209).

The poor state of its conservation later led Gustavo Frizzoni both to complain about the absence of a portrait in the Pinacoteca Comunale Martinengo "that would worthily represent the importance of Moretto in such types of painting", and to accept "its attribution to Bonvicino not without hesitation" (1889, p. 31). The same negative interpretation was made by Giovanni Morelli, who judged it the "work of imitators of Moretto" (1890, p. 374), while Pietro Da Ponte cautiously returned the painting to Moretto (1898, p. 41).

In the twentieth century the portrait was firmly attributed by all critics to Moretto, with suggested dates ranging from 1535 to 1545. Giorgio Nicodemi placed it with works painted by Moretto between 1540 and 1545 for "the maestro's way of portraying fabrics", and added that "this portrait must certainly come within" the same years (1927, p. 60). Adolfo Venturi in 1929 (pp. 140, 202) for the first time likened the work to a group of portraits by Moretto influenced by Lotto, such as the *Portrait of a Young Man* in London (National Gallery), the *Portrait of a Man of Science* in Genoa (Palazzo Rosso) and the *Priest* in Munich (Alte Pinakothek). This was then taken up by Camillo Boselli, who also noted that the painting anticipated Moroni's portraiture (1954, pp. 103, 134). Defined by Rossana Bossaglia (1963, p. 1083) as a "certain" painting by Moretto, Panazza studied the relationship between Bonvicino and Lotto more closely and found future influences on Moroni and Caravaggio: "a congenial affinity, a link that can not easily be said to be direct or due to similar moods, to a parallelism of temperament or style, are evident between the inspired Venetian painter and the more serene, placid Brescian"; and "the painting is an expressive, colorful, characteristic Venetian portrait. But it is made extremely personal by Moretto, primarily by the ray of light that crosses the canvas creating precious silken reflections on the rosy garment and plastically molding the figure. It is a typical solution used by Moretto, which was then to be developed by Moroni, until given a tragic intensity and sudden revelation in Caravaggio" (1958, p. 125; 1968, pp. 127, 227).

In his monograph on the painter for the Brescia exhibition *Alessandro Bonvicino. Il Moretto* (1988), Pier Virgilio Begni Redona suggested a date between 1535 and 1540, close to the *Altarpiece* at Sant'Andrea in Bergamo from 1536 and the Rovellio *Altarpiece* in the Pinacoteca Tosio Martinengo dated 1539 (1988, pp. 306–307).

In 1535 Moretto is known to have briefly frequented the court of Isabella d'Este (Frati, 1898, p. 354; Begni Redona, 1988, p. 597). In 1540–41 he painted works for some Verona churches and a portrait of Aretino, mentioned in a letter from that writer to Giorgio Vasari in 1543 (Begni Redona, 1988, pp. 598–601). At this stage of his career Moretto was eager to establish new links with Venetian culture and intellectual circles, and these influenced his work at least until the early 1540s. The Venetian style of the painting is mainly evident in the composition and coloring. The latter is only slightly toned down by a specifically Lombard use of light, low on the surfaces and atmospheric in the background. This allows the gentleman to be likened to the *Tullia of Aragon*, painted by Moretto around 1537, and to other portraits of obvious Venetian influence, such as the *Lady in the Garden* from ca. 1536 (Brescia, Palazzo Salvadego) and the *Portrait of a Man* of 1540 (Brescia, private collection, see Begni Redona, 1988, pp. 334–335), distinguished by Venetian elements and an accentuated brightness and silkiness of the fabrics.

Compared to the greater openness of those works, Moretto placed this gentleman in an enclosed, clearly defined place, probably a study, bordered by a grey frame that acts as a window. Through this the observer can more easily "focus" the subject in his moment of privacy. This makes the work very natural and, despite the frontal pose of the subject, movement is suggested by the position of the right hand holding the letter. The gentleman's "fashionable" clothing and the coloring of the scene, all played out on pink, green and black, allow this portrait to be compared to Titian's 1538 portrait of *Francesco I*, now in the Louvre, and therefore dated to about the same year.

As noted in the nineteenth century, the painting is not in very good condition, impaired in some places by restoration and retouching (around the eyes and in the background). This was probably carried out in the nineteenth century by its owner, Alessandro Sala, who also carried out supplementary restorations to Moretto's *Assumption* in the Duomo Vecchio around the middle of the century.

Massimiliano Capella

Alessandro Bonvicino called Moretto da Brescia

(Brescia ca. 1498–1554)

Pentecost

ca. 1542–45
Oil on canvas; 98 x 65 3/4 in. (249 x 167 cm)
Inv. 79

Provenance: Brescia, church of San Giuseppe, ninth chapel on the right, until at least 1826; then moved to third chapel on the right, 1834; Brescia, Pinacoteca Comunale Tosio, 1869; Brescia, Pinacoteca Tosio Martinengo, 1906.
Restoration: 1988, Marchetti & Fontanini, Brescia.

This "fine, carefully made painting by Moretto" (Faino, 1630–69, ed. 1961, p. 94) has been noted among the artistic treasures of the Franciscan church of San Giuseppe since the earliest guides to Brescia. Construction of the church began in 1519 and by 1539 work had begun on its floors and those of its chapels, according to a sixteenth-century note by Fassino (*Registro*, f. 270v). The big *Pentecost* altarpiece was originally above the altar of the ninth chapel on the right dedicated to the Holy Spirit.

The chapels were assigned to Brescian noble families like the Avogadro and the Calini; that of the Holy Spirit probably went to the Zone and Mussi families (Volta, 1989, p. 27), but there is no confirmation of this. Their decoration then led to commissions for various artists, primarily Romanino and Moretto. The latter first painted the altarpiece for the chapel assigned in 1526 to Bishop Mattia Ugoni. This important clergyman had promoted construction of the new church and supported Moretto with commissions for other works (Agosti, Zani, 1992): the *Archangel Michael* for the Luzzago chapel, on the left of the main altar, and the *Pentecost*.

Both works were to be taken to the Pinacoteca di Brera in Milan after closure of the convent of San Giuseppe in 1810, but remained in place thanks to the Prefect of the Dipartimento del Mella and the Minister of the Interior (Prestini, 1989, pp. 146–147). The *Pentecost* was moved to the third chapel on the right during a general reorganization of the church that took place

between publication of the Brognoli guide in 1826 and the Sala guide in 1834. The church and convent were closed and taken into state ownership in 1866, and the "panel", as it was described, moved to the Pinacoteca Comunale of Brescia (Prestini, 1989, pp. 159–160). It was accompanied by two other paintings by Moretto (*Virgin with St Michael and St Francis* and the detached fresco of *Christ Falling under the Weight of the Cross*) and three by Romanino (*Nativity*, *Pietà* and *St Paul and Saints Jerome, John the Baptist, Mary Magdalene and Catherine of Alexandria*) (Gianfranceschi, Lucchesi Ragni, 2006, pp. 82–89).

A document dated 19 March 1914 in the Brescia civic museums archive (inv. 79) shows that on 13 December 1869 a receipt was issued to the Head of Crown Property by the Pinacoteca Comunale Tosio "for the successful transfer" of the *Pentecost* and the other paintings from San Giuseppe. This was part of a complex negotiation begun in 1913 by the director Giulio Zappa to obtain the monumental wooden frame of the altarpiece, which had "remained in the third altar on the right in San Giuseppe". The frame was finally placed on deposit in the Pinacoteca in September 1914 thanks to the intervention of the local revenue office. The art gallery then appointed the painter Vittorio Trainini to restore the chapel, where a sixteenth-century fresco had been discovered.

The official delivery document of 26 October 1914 carries the following report: "the Pinacoteca notes that the frame is in poor condition, missing some of its beading, several pieces of inlay and the entire base". Its restoration was carried out the following year by the gilder Angelo Poisa.

Some work was also carried out on the painting at

that time, identified during Luisa Marchetti and Alberto Fontanini's 1988 restoration for the Moretto exhibition. The original canvas in four sections sewn together had been relined with paste and the edges plastered and touched up, mainly in the bottom right corner.

The careful description of the painting made by Francesco Paglia in the seventeenth-century (ed. Boselli, 1967, p. 102) emphasized the eloquence of the figures, beginning with the "great modesty of that immaculate and ever Virgin Mary, all beauty, grace and majesty, and the expressive, natural effects of those Apostles, all filled with joy". Such expressiveness was derived from the naturalism typical of Lombard painting, with its movement of body and spirit, and given "such noble and harmonious arrangement, in form, color and design: with architecture so realistic it has a wonderful effect". The classical approach, focused on the reality of things and with an almost forced showiness, was interpreted by Moretto "with sublime and heroic intelligence". Paglia ends by giving the work a Venetian influence through the most prestigious comparison possible: "and it resembles Titian".

Such comments seem an early anticipation of Longhi (1929, p. 271), who noted "Lombard qualities" and placed the *Pentecost* among Caravaggio's influences. Moretto "seems to take up the architectural structure of Bellini, Cima etc., but, now indifferent to that constructive rigor, uses the votive framing to present new effects of intense, typically Lombard Illusionism, obtained not with the mystery of old perspective, but with a more grazing light and the invention of forms that seem to suddenly emerge from the painting". The emphasis was no longer only on realism, but on new formal studies of light, space and expression: "Here in the *Pentecost* is the shadow that lines the marble floor three times; here are the two apostles in the foreground, or rather outside the foreground, resting beyond the furthest pilaster; moreover, contrary to all decorum, showing off the soles of their bare feet".

Some reservations were expressed about the painting's attribution, starting with Crowe and Cavalcaselle (1871, p. 413) and Frizzoni (1889, p. 31), who noted academic aspects and a certain formal, chromatic heaviness. But Longhi banished such comments with his greater knowledge of Moretto's work. Lechi and Panazza (*La pittura bresciana…*, 1939, p. 87) pointed to Titian's

Pentecost in Santa Maria della Salute in Venice as the model for the altarpiece, implicitly suggesting a date in the 1540s. Gombosi (1943, pp. 16, 32), however, proposed the 1520s, relating the work to the Sant'Eufemia altarpiece, while Boselli (1954, pp. 105, 136) preferred 1540–44, his dating for the *Supper in the House of the Pharisee* in the Museo Diocesano of Venice.

A date of 1543–44 was then established (Begni Redona, 1988, pp. 392–394, also for the bibliography), despite the frame having been attributed to Stefano Lamberti who had died in 1538, though such attribution is not confirmed (Bayer, in *Alessandro Bonvicino…*, 1988, pp. 251–252).

Four x-rays made of the altarpiece during the 1988 restorations confirmed its generally good condition (Stradiotti, in *Alessandro Bonvicino…*, 1988, p. 219). A first draft of the Virgin's face at the height of her neck has suggested that the figure was "originally conceived nearer the center" and then "moved back to create greater depth".

The painting is particularly noted for its perspective. This is emphasized by the wooden framing of the altarpiece and its original position in the shallow chapel of San Giuseppe, whose arch it continues in greater depth. Titian's *Pentecost* (which replaced the first version of 1541 painted for Santo Spirito in Isola and is now in the Basilica della Salute in Venice) influenced the new direction taken by Moretto in the 1540s. His new Mannerist style was partly inspired by the presence in Venice of Salviati and Vasari, but mainly "in the influence of this presence on Venetian painters, first and foremost on Titian" (Ballarin, in *Le siècle di Titien*, 1993, p. 425). There is also a more marked use of illusion. The figures are brought closer with that light and movement so typical of Moretto's work, though here restrained to reveal a deeper truth. The shadows lengthen on the floor and seem to disappear, but thicken on the apostles at the right. They almost blur some of the faces, in contrast with the silken splendor of the illuminated clothing, from the vivid yellows, blues and whites in the foreground to the iridescent pink of the Virgin.

The movements of the figures are expressed both in their physical form and expressions, recalling Moretto's paintings for the church of San Giovanni Evangelista in Brescia in the 1520s. He reinterpreted these with the

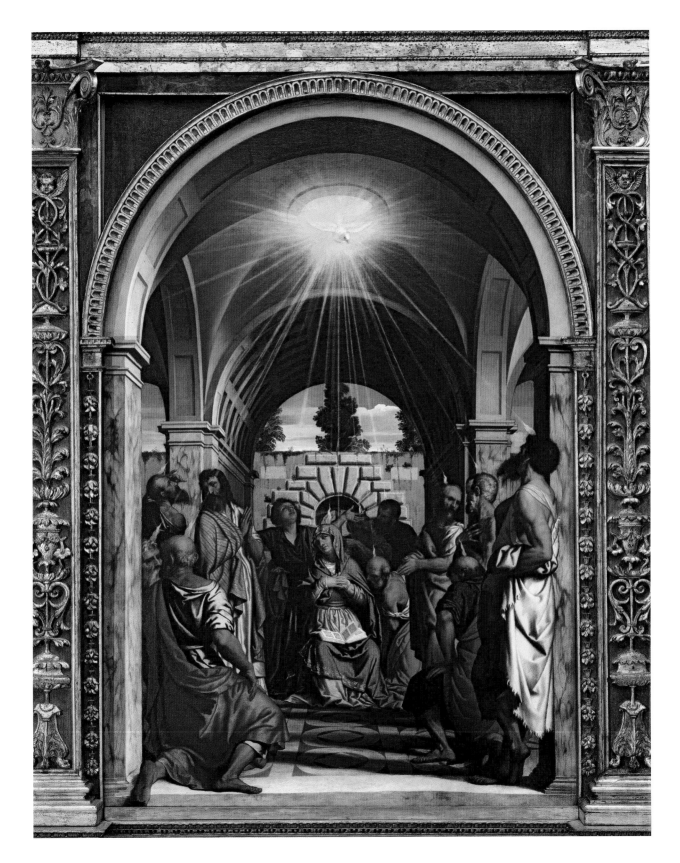

new Mannerist approach in his paintings for the chapel of San Giovanni Evangelista, towards 1543. They have been justifiably compared to the altarpiece and organ shutters in the same church (Ballarin, in *Le siècle di Titien*, 1993, p. 425).

The architecture of the altarpiece, which has been likened to the work of Sanmicheli (Zani, in *Alessandro Bonvicino...*, 1988, pp. 289–290), also documents this change. Its austerity and liturgical solemnity reflect the severity of the prevailing religious climate (Guazzoni, in *Alessandro Bonvicino...*, 1988, p. 264). But Moretto always demonstrated a deep religious faith. The supernatural light of the Holy Spirit charges the painting made of light and shade and deepens the human truth it reveals.

Marco Rossi

Luca Mombello

(Orzivecchi ca. 1518/20–Brescia? after 1592)

Immaculate Conception and a King

late 16th century
Oil on canvas; 34 5/8 x 31 1/4 in. (88 x 79.5 cm)
Inv. 107

Provenance: Brescia, Palazzo della Loggia, until at least 1853; Brescia, Pinacoteca Comunale Tosio, from 1863 to 1888; Brescia, Pinacoteca Comunale Martinengo, from 1888 to 1906; Brescia, Pinacoteca Tosio Martinengo, since 1906.
Restoration: 1994, Romeo Seccamani, Brescia.

Still in its precious original frame, the painting is one of the more characteristic examples of Mombello's late work. It has all the signs of the decorative and devotional decline that typified his painting from the 1550s and '60s. The absence of a signature, a date or any relevant documents, as for many of the other small or medium-size works given to him, makes a precise dating difficult, though attribution here is certain. The original location of the work is unknown, but in the first half of the nineteenth century it was owned by the city council and exhibited in the Palazzo della Loggia in Brescia, alongside masterpieces by Moretto. Brognoli (1826, p. 63) mentioned two paintings by Mombello "in the third room, at the sides of the window in the entrance facade", though without specifying their subject, while Alessandro Sala (1834, p. 100) and Federico Odorici (1853, p. 151), misunderstood the subjects, recalling "an Annunciation" and a "Holy Triad". According to the Pinacoteca's documentation, however, the only two works by Mombello that came from the Palazzo della Loggia were this *Immaculate Conception* and a *Coronation of the Virgin with Allegories of Modesty and Humility* (inv. 695). The latter did not arrive until the end of the century, while the former had already been referred to by Odorici in the printed catalog (1863, p. 17) and subsequent manuscript inventory by Tommaso Castellini (1868, p. 38 no. 185). It must therefore have been transferred in the previous decade, possibly not long after those of Moretto in 1853.

The failure to understand the theme of the painting is not surprising given the variety of titles under which it has been recorded. Strangely, but not without iconographic reason, Odorici and Castellini defined it as *The Fountain of the Holy Spirit*, applying to the Virgin the symbol of the fountain seen behind her. Camillo Boselli (in Boselli-Panazza 1946, p. 99) subsequently recorded it as the *Temptation of the Serpent*, with an evident misunderstanding and slippage of meaning, despite the theme having already been correctly interpreted by Giorgio Nicodemi (1927, p. 43) as the *Immaculate Conception*. This title was taken up later by Boselli himself (1953, p. 14) and by Gaetano Panazza (1959, p. 70). The matter was complicated in subsequent inventories and studies due to the royal figure beside the Virgin being identified as David. This resulted in Luciano Anelli (1978, p. 70) discussing the *Blessed Virgin and Child with David in the Garden of Eden*, before going back to the old title of *The Temptation of the Serpent* (1988a, pp. 80, 84); Bruno Passamani's *Guida* also refers to David (1988, p. 73).

There are two distinct iconographic themes in the painting, the *hortus conclusus* (enclosed garden) and the Garden of Eden, whose crossover is the basis of the misunderstandings. Nicodemi had already recognized the king at the left as the Eternal Father, who contemplates and presents the masterpiece of his creation, the Blessed Virgin. The work is constructed as a kind of theological riddle and reflects the doctrinal leanings of the painter, translated in a studied and slightly lifeless piety. The Tree of Knowledge in the center of the painting is no longer encircled by the serpent, but by a reassuring garland of bluebells, while the traditional tempter finds itself crushed beneath the feet of Mary, the Second Eve. The association of the Blessed Virgin with the tree and serpent had already appeared in Vasari's *Allegory* (Anelli, 1978), though resolved in different terms. The Virgin is also the Woman of the Apocalypse who saves the Child from the beast, which is why Mombello presents Mary with the Child in her arms, held above the serpent. A flowering field of narcissus and lily of the valley extends around them with birds and animals, including a unicorn. The whole context seems to refer to the Garden of Eden, as confirmed by the monumental door in the background, watched over by St Michael Archangel with sword in hand. But the perfumed flowers, the palm and especially the complicated fountain in the background with caryatids and masks, even a statue of a female faun who squirts water from her breasts, refer to the *hortus conclusus*, the *fons signata* and the *puteus aquarum viventium* of the *Cantico dei Cantici*. In another composition that is certainly by Mombello, in the chancellery of the sanctuary of Santa Maria delle Grazie in Brescia, the Virgin is presented in the *hortus conclusus*, though placed between the sun and moon ("beautiful as the moon, brilliant as the sun") and the emblems of the *Litanie lauretane* (see also Anelli 1981, p. 292). In the Pinacoteca Tosio Martinengo painting, Mary is therefore seen on one hand as the Second Eve and on the other as the bride of the Canticles, contemplated by Solomon "adorned in his crown". The latter, the bridegroom of the Canticles, represents the Holy Father.

The complicated theological symbolism is even taken up in the frame, certainly contemporary with and specifically made for the painting. The flowers and fruit obviously relate to the theme of the *hortus* (garden), while the tree carved in the middle of the upper band, between two large volutes, repeats the one at the center of the painting and emphasizes its *arbor vitae* meaning.

The frame is so closely linked to the painting by its iconography and matching decorative flowers that it was probably made by Mombello. However, the tradition that he was Moretto's "frame maker" who devoted himself to painting only later is unfounded. Camillo Boselli (1949) claimed to have seen documents in the Brescia chapter archive that documented this profession, but these remain unpublished. So the only proof at present is the elaborate frames, of a vaguely provincial and flamboyant opulence, that are still on some of his paintings. These include an *Annunciation* in a private Brescia collection, where the rich frieze with carved leaves curves above in a delicately perforated cyma with blossoming gilt branches and purple rosettes, and a *Coronation of the Virgin* in the chapel of the Nuvolera cemetery (near Brescia), noted by Anelli (1988, p. 69; see Anelli 1992, p. 34 n. 18).

This particular frame is an extraordinarily enriched variant of the Veneto and Sansovino model (as noted by Patrizia Zambrano in *La cornice*, 1992, pp. 160–161). A complex weave of overlapping volutes and garlands includes heads with glass paste eyes; some with busts and pot bellies resemble figureheads. In some places the curve springs from a straight element like the neck of a viola or other string instrument. The detailed decorations carved along the crest or on the sides of the volutes and the touches of color (blue for the berries, red for some flowers) seem to anticipate the sumptuous, heavy Brescian designs of the late sixteenth century and the Baroque age. The frame is an integral part of this singular devotional "object" and, after its restoration in 1993–94, along with the painting, is now more effectively shown off in all its material richness, including its rich gilding.

Despite the uncertain chronology of Mombello's work, particularly from the later period when there was a notable absence of development, the painting can only be given a fairly late dating. This would place it close to the *Madonna of the Rosary* in Prevalle (Brescia), from 1589, and similar works such as the two altarpieces in the church of Santi Cosma e Damiano or the *Blessed Virgin and Saints* in Barzaniga, in the province of Cremona (but originally in the Dominican church in Brescia; see Guazzoni, 1996, pp. 275–282). These are all diminished by obvious signs of weakening composition and decoration (Rossana Bossaglia spoke of "trinkets", 1963, p. 1083, regarding the Pinacoteca Martinengo painting), but redeemed by their archaistic candor and an appealing, almost courtly Gothic tone.

Valerio Guazzoni

Giovanni Battista Moroni

(Albino, Bergamo ca. 1520–Bergamo 1579)

St Faustinus

ca. 1545–50
Oil on panel; 11 5/8 x 6 1/4 in. (29.5 x 16 cm)
Annotation on the back: *42*
Inv. 125

St Jovita

ca. 1545–50
Oil on panel; 11 5/8 x 6 1/4 in. (29.5 x 16 cm)
Annotation on the back: *43*
Inv. 126

Provenance: Brescia, Paolo Tosio collection; City of Brescia bequeathed by Paolo Tosio, 1844; Brescia, Pinacoteca Tosio, from 1851 to 1906; Brescia, Pinacoteca Tosio Martinengo from 1906. *Restoration*: 2005, Romeo Seccamani, Brescia.

Although the two paintings on oak panels are in good condition, the recent restoration has revealed limited pigment loss in the darker background. However, what has emerged in particular, is the painter's extraordinary skill. This can be appreciated both in the freely applied flowing dark outline of the two figures, and in the considerable freshness of the palette. Delicate chromatic nuances are visible in the pink-mauve of the sandals, in the rose-colored transparent layers, applied on the drapery and banners, and in the golden highlights of the armor.

At the edge of the panels there is an unpainted strip about 5mm wide, which corresponds to the area originally covered by a small wooden frame. A few traces of its golding remain at the edges of the picture's surface. At the back of the panel there are some grooves that must have been used to fit the painting into a larger structure. They consist of a rectangular notch in the middle part of the top side, and a vertical groove on the lower side. The figures "42" (in no. 125) and "43" (in no. 126) are inscribed on the back of the panels.

Not much is known about the history of the two paintings prior to 1844, nor is there any information about the circumstances in which they were purchased by the Brescia collector Paolo Tosio.

In Tosio's earliest inventory (*Riepilogo…*, 1844 63, 64), the paintings were ascribed to "Morone d'Albino", with reference to Giovanni Battista Moroni. The attribution to the Bergamo artist was reconfirmed in an ensuing list (*Oggetti d'arte…*, 1846, f. 4, no. 88); but later, in the first printed catalog of the gallery in 1854, it was replaced by attribution to "Marone", referring to the painter Pietro Marone, from Brescia (Odorici, 1854, p. 15, no. 151). It is not clear whether the change can be ascribed to a conscious decision, or to a mere misunderstanding due to the similarity of the names. Apart from an inventory made in 1864 (*Catalogue…*, 1864, nos. 63, 64), once again suggesting the name of Moroni, all the subsequent nineteenth-century catalogs of the gallery–both hand-written and printed–attribute the two paintings to Pietro Marone (Odorici, 1863, p. 11, no. 101; Castellini, 1868, f. 32; Ariassi, 1875, f. 13; Odorici, 1879, p. 21, nos. 50, 51; Odorici, 1888, p. 23, nos. 23, 24). The repeated attribution to Marone has affected modern research so much so that the reference has been unanimously confirmed (because of inertia) and reasserted, not only in all publications about the gallery until quite recently (Nicodemi, 1927, p. 50; Panazza, Boselli, 1974, p. 127; Passamani, 1988, p. 73), but also in many essays on the painter (Panazza, Boselli, 1946, p. 145; Begni Redona 1964, p. 527). The references also include the page Adolfo Venturi (1938, p. 352) dedicated to the painter Marone, in which both the panels are reproduced bearing a brief inscription that considers them evidence of Moretto's influence on Pietro Marone.

The paintings depict two saints dressed in armor, placed in an extremely sober setting, defined only by the base on which the two figures stand. Both carry the palm of martyrdom and a white banner, held respectively in their left and right hands, and wear a cloak fastened at the shoulder. The identification of the two saints as the patron saints of Brescia Faustinus and Jovita was suggested for the first time by Giorgio Nicodemi (1927, p. 50) and accepted unanimously thereafter, as it appeared to be substantially compatible with the iconographic data of the two figures. It matched the traditional representation of the two martyred brothers as soldiers and ombudsmen of the city, popular from the beginning of the late 1400s. Because of the rather generic iconography of the characters, and their lack of distinctive details, a margin of uncertainty still remains in their identification. Moreover, the identical characterization of the two saints, both with beard, clashes with the common practice of distinguishing the older Faustinus from his brother (regarding this, see the altarpiece in the church of Sarezzo, a late production of the Moretto workshop in which unlike Jovita, Faustinus is depicted with a beard; Begni Redona, 1988, pp. 504, 505).

However, the superb quality of the paintings fully revealed with the recent restoration, has made us at long last, reassess the two panels which have previously not been the specific subject of study. The first appropriate observation is that the attribution to Pietro Marone (Manerbio? 1548-Brescia 1603) which has nearly always accompanied these two paintings, is unfounded. It was based more on the belief, disproven above, that the painting was originally attributed to him by the Tosio collection itself, than on the analysis of their distinctive style. Marone, who probably came originally from Manerbio, was one of the most important protagonists of the Brescian art scene in the last three decades of the sixteenth century. He stands out for his pictorial language based on a mature Mannerist style, driven by a powerful command of drawing and by strong theatrical staging based on a close study of the paintings of Veronese. These characteristics are not present in the two panels which relate to what was happening in Brescia in the 1550's, that was earlier and less eccentric than the context in which Marone lived and worked.

It cannot be overlooked how close the two paintings are to the style of Moretto in their pure, direct Naturalism and the meticulous, almost tender, chiaroscuro. Comparison to Moretto's *Christ at the Column* in the Naples Capodimonte Museum places them in the same time frame. The Capodimonte picture is a masterpiece of Moretto's late maturity and a sort of noble father to our two standard-bearer saints.

Identifying this decisive source cannot on the other hand stop us from perceiving the subtle but detectable difference between the two martyrs and Moretto's pictorial language. It is not so much a question of lesser quality, as a more descriptive pictorial language. The use of the tip of the brush transforms the airy and broad formal concept of the Brescian painter into a tighter and more graphic approach, which accounts for the elongated and slim build of the two saints. However, more importantly, these particular features correspond to the distinctive interpretation of Moretto's models by his best pupil, Giovanni Battista Moroni, from Bergamo, who trained in Moretto's workshop of the brescian artist during the 1540s. There are consistent similarities between these two panels and many of the works of the earlier and more Moretto-like phase of Moroni's career. The execution is quite similar, both in the fluid and smooth depiction of the saints' immaculate banners–resembling the drapery of *Christ Resurrected* (in the cathedral of Bergamo) and the small privately owned *Crucifix* (Gregori, 1979[1], p. 316, no. 216)–and in the reflections rendered with parallel strokes to enhance the saints' armor. This technique had already been used by Moretto (in the two angels of the polyptych formerly in Gardone Valtrompia; reproduced in *La pittura del '500…*, 1988, pp. 74, 75). It was subsequently applied by Moroni first in his early drawings, of which some are dated 1543. These were directly taken from his Master's models (Litta, 2004). He then used them in several of his first paintings, such as the

Giovanni Battista Moroni
Angel at Prayer
private collection

Giovanni Battista Moroni
Angel at Prayer
private collection

Mystic Marriage of St Catherine at the Ashmolean Museum, in Oxford and *St Agnes* at the Columbus Gallery of Fine Arts. If we were to add that the similarity of facial type and gesture of the two characters, notably of the saint no. 126, to the *St John the Evangelist* conceived by Moroni during his early years and used in a drawing in the the Brescia Gallery, in the related altarpiece of the Orzivecchi parish, and in the church of Santa Maria Maggiore in Trento (1551–52), I believe the grounds on which to attribute the two panels to the Bergamo artist are totally convincing.

It is clear, in this context, that attribution of the paintings to Moroni when they were in the Paolo Tosio collection supports my observations; above all if one considers that, most probably, the old attribution was not made by some enlightened expert ahead of his time, but must have been based on objective information or at least on historical tradition.

At this stage however, it is best to clarify that the stylistic analysis of the two panels, with relevant hypothesis about their context, has been further confirmed by the identification of three related works. I'm referring, first of all, to a small panel portraying the *Prophet Elijah* (in the Musée d'Art et d'Histoire in Cognac). This painting has already been ascribed to Moroni, in the critical references that culminated in the publication of the painting as part of the essay by Mina Gregori, who dates the painting to the 1550s (1979[1], p. 254, no. 94).

The Cognac panel is the same size as the two Tosio saints (29.5 x 17 cm) and not only re-confirms the distinctive qualities of the pictorial language, but also the manner of presenting the figure and its austere spacial setting, including the exquisite rendition of the flickering shadow on the right. These elements confirm its association to the two Brescian paintings. Consequently, the secure assignment of the French panel to Moroni confirms the hypothesis of attribution suggested above. The Cognac painting seems to give further evidence in favor of its execution at a stage of the painter's career still strongly marked by Moretto's teachings. The inscription on the large slate held by the prophet refers to the Eucharist ("HIC / EST / PANIS /

QUI DE / CELO / DESCEN/DIT"; John, 6, 33). The writing resembles the captions inserted regularly by Moretto in his late works. In the case of Eucharistic excerpts, the grape vine motif was added and placed at the end of the text (see the slate held by King Solomon in the *Christ in Passion with Moses and Solomon*, executed by Moretto for the church of Santi Nazaro and Celsio, in Brescia, between 1541 and 1542).

The other two associated paintings depict *Angels at Prayer*, and are privately owned. So far they have had a brief historiography (Begni Redona, 1988, p. 532; Penny, 2004, p. 170). They are thought to derive from two panels of the same theme in the National Gallery, London, ascribed to Moretto, at times to his workshop. These panels were originally set on the inside part of an altarpiece, whose original location is unknown (see Penny, 2004, pp. 167–171 about the outside cover of the London panels depicting St Joseph and St Jerome).

The two *Angels at Prayer* also have similar measurements (29.5 x 16 cm) to the two Brescian saints. To dispel any remaining doubts, the framework at the back of the *Angel at Prayer* turned to the right has the same grooves as the Tosio panels, used for fitting the painting into a common structure.

The stylistic similarities linking the angels to the other three works can be appreciated in details like the parallel strokes of golden lighting on the two figures' dark garments, which repeat the technical devices used for the knight-saints.

Moreover, the fact that the panels in the private collection mimic the two London Moretto-like angels, reinforces our hypothesis, especially since Moroni had had plenty of opportunities to copy his Master's work in his earlier years, depicting Moretto's models with the more descriptive and graphic pictorial style.

This practice of appropriation was never uncritical, which is exactly what distinguishes the two small paintings under consideration. The broad, monumental approach of the London prototypes is here expressed with more analytical and miniaturistic traits, exemplified by the addition of several captious details that do not appear in the models, such as the complicated system of folds that moves the angels' cloaks, or the knotted fringe motif that decorates their golden highlighted gowns.

On the other hand, the soft purity of the faces and the

Giovanni Battista Moroni
The Prophet Elijah
Cognac, Musée d'Art et d'Histoire

blooming consistency of the flesh leave no doubt that the two *Angels at Prayer* belong to that part of Moroni's production where Moretto's influence is most evident.

This obviously supports the hypothesis that all five works were executed at a very early date, maybe around the 1540s. Further evidence is provided by the presence among these images of the Saints Faustinus and Jovita, a sure sign that the whole series was a Brescian commission. This induces us to date the works to the period when Moroni was still part of that context.

The attempt to provide more precise information on the matter clashes with the well known difficulty of reconstructing the beginning of the painter's career. So far, the only proof has been provided by the above mentioned drawings of 1543, taken from Moretto prototypes, which, besides being the first definite chronological reference in Moroni's career–who was in his early twenties at the time–allow us to firmly establish that he was present in Moretto's workshop.

Bearing this in mind, the lack of paintings definitely dated prior to the works produced in Trento (1548 and in 1551–52), makes it difficult to ascertain the exact dynamics of the artist's "debut".

There has not yet been the occasion called for by Gregori (1979[2], p. 41) for a close examination of the prolific production of Moretto's workshop during the 1540s. It could eventually clarify the exact role Moroni had in that context, (a first attempt has been made by Gregori, 1979[1], pp. 290–292, no. 167; see Guerini, 1986, pp. 17–19 and Guzzo, 1988, pp. 27–31 for different views on the matter) and whose involvement with Moretto and the Brescian setting must have lasted at least until 1549; a fact that can be proved by an important document dating from the same year.

While awaiting a crucial analysis of the five panels we can only emphasize that they must have been produced after the panels of the Moretto workshop, now in London, from which Moroni seems to have taken not only the subject matter–the two *Angels at Prayer*–but also the idea of setting all the figures on a short white marble base. However this does not provide a date because the Moretto altar panels also lack a specific time reference.

These difficulties are compensated, at least in part, by more definite remarks that can be made about the original function of the five panels. As has been suggested in the comments about the two *Angels at Prayer* and the *Prophet Elijah* (Penny, 2004, p. 170; Gregori, 1979[1], p. 254, no. 94; Rossi, 1980, pp. 129–131), they may be the only remains of the pictorial decoration of a wooden tabernacle, whose original location is not difficult to imagine.

The hypothesis about this original position can be confirmed both by the clear reference to the Eucharist theme, seen in the inscriptions on the Cognac panel, and by the presence of the two *Angels at Prayer*. Their side view conforms with the iconographic tradition of tabernacle decoration, according to which the figures should be arranged directly on the side of the panel that opened to access the Eucharist.

Although the extreme variety of church furnishings (see *Suppellettili ecclesiastiche*, 1988, pp. 84–90) counsels caution, we may suppose that the tabernacle to which the paintings belonged was a temple-like structure, not very different from the one in San Fiastrio di Tavernole (now in the Pinacoteca Tosio Martinengo, inv. 962) whose panels were decorated by Francesco Ricchino in 1568.

It is clear that, if the panels were to have been set in a small construction with a hexagonal plan, such as the one decorated by Ricchino, the only missing part of the whole would be the central panel, which could have had a

Eucharistic image or a scene from the Passion, or an image of the Resurrection of Christ: the theme chosen for a painting with the same function, executed by young Moroni himself, in the Bergamo Cathedral (Gregori, 1979[1], p. 235, no. 39).

If the size difference compared to the other works of the series does not allow this last panel to be associated to the group partly re-united here, there is no doubt that the tabernacle panel of the Bergamo Cathedral provides very useful evidence, as it shows the painter's familiarity with this type of production. Moroni must have decorated other tabernacles. The two *Angels at Prayer* in the Museo Diocesano, Bergamo, and the *Angel at Prayer* at the Indiana University of Bloomington, (Gregori, 1979[1], p. 234, nos. 36, 37; p. 243, no. 64) were probably placed similarly to the two panels of the same theme analyzed here.

Additional information is provided in a 1567 document recording Moroni's commission. To all this information, it is best to add that which is provided in an important document of 1567, where a commission is recorded to the artist for several paintings, to be placed in the now lost tabernacle of the curch of Sant'Alessandro in Colonna, in Bergamo (Gregori, 1979[1], p. 108). Further, the reference in Giacomo Carrara's inventory for his Bergamo collection, compiled in 1796, lists two matching panels by Moroni, now lost, respectively depicting a *Prophet* and a *Resurrected Christ* which, as previously suggested (Rossi, 1980), could also have been part of that tabernacle. If we could identify the *Prophet* in the Carrara inventory with the one now in Cognac, it would be inevitable to recognize the *Christ Resurrected*, previously in the same collection, as the missing panel in our series.

Francesco Frangi

Giovanni Battista Moroni

(Albino, Bergamo ca. 1520–Bergamo 1579)

Portrait of a Man of Letters (The Magistrate)

1560
Oil on canvas; 45 7/8 x 36 in. (116 x 91.5 cm)
Inscription on the letter held by the figure:
Aquí quedo con sossiego; the letter begins:

Mag.co Seg.r Etore L...., ..., and is dated at the
bottom: XX FEBR. M.D.LX. It is signed by the artist:
Gi: Bat.a Morone pit.e Albin.
Inv. 147

Provenance: Brescia, Avoltori collection; Brescia, Paolo Tosio collection, prior to 1826 and until 1844; Comune di Brescia, by bequest of Paolo Tosio, 1844; Brescia, Pinacoteca Comunale Tosio, from 1851 to 1906; Brescia, Pinacoteca Tosio Martinengo, since 1906.
Restoration: 1956, Ottemi Della Rotta, Milan.

A comprehensive history of the collecting of Moroni's works has yet to be written. But it is known that the artist's paintings began to gradually circulate, even beyond the Bergamo area, from an early date. His works went into various Brescian collections, where sources indicate paintings other than this *Magistrate*. In 1826 Brognoli noted it as being in the Avoltori collection prior to its purchase by Paolo Tosio (Brognoli, 1826, p. 332). Tosio's other works of Brescian origin included the *Portrait of M. A. Savelli* (Lisbon, Gulbelkian museum), owned first by Uggeri, then Teodoro Lechi; the *Canon Ludovico di Terzi* (London, National Gallery), which went into Luigi Avogadro's collection and then into the home of the Fenaroli counts; the *Bust of a Prelate with Beret* (Florence, Pitti Palace), purchased in Cremona in 1668 for Cardinal Leopoldo de' Medici but originally from Brescia; the *Portrait of a Man Holding a Letter* (London, National Gallery), also listed among the estate of Teodoro Lechi, along with the *Two Donors in Adoration before the Madonna and Child and St Michael* (Richmond, Virginia, Museum of Fine Arts) and the *Portrait of Don Gabriel de la Cueva y Girón, Duke of Alburquerque* (Berlin, Gemäldegalerie); see the entries by Mina Gregori in Giovan Battista Moroni (1979, pp. 24–25, 70, 118, 126, 129, 186, 210, with previous bibliography; but for the numerous Moroni works formerly owned by Lechi, see also Lechi, 1968, ad indicem). The geographical and cultural proximity of Bergamo and Brescia, and Moroni's training with Moretto

(attested by Ridolfi from 1648) are not enough to explain this phenomenon. Possibly inspired by the numerous Moroni works chosen by Teodoro Lechi, Paolo Tosio acquired the *Magistrate* and the painting of the so-called *Unknown Poet*. He bought these two excellent examples of Moroni's mature portraiture at precisely the time the international market was beginning to get enthusiastic about his work. The high number of Moroni works in early Brescian art collections prompted Gregori to cautiously suggest that the artist may have spent some time in Brescia at the end of the 1550s, when there is no mention of him in Albino and Bergamo documents (Gregori, 1979[1], p. 298.)

Roberto Longhi's admiration for this work is evident in the entry for the *Portrait of the Unknown Poet*: from its very early mention in his 1911 essay (Longhi, 1995, p. 25) through to its presentation at the 1953 exhibition *I pittori della realtà in Lombardia* (1953, 14, p. 27), he considered the so-called *Portrait of a Magistrate* as being characteristic of the artist, whose typically Brescian naturalism immediately caught the eye of the great scholar.

In 1929 Adolfo Venturi noted "the powerful emphasis [and] great fluidity of brush" in the *Magistrate*, which he dated, along with the contemporary *Unknown Poet*, to the artist's maturity (IX, p. 227); Gertrud Lendorff also mentioned the portrait, in 1933 (p. 27).

Moroni was given important critical attention in 1979 with publication of the monograph by Mina Gregori, who with Francesco Rossi also curated the Bergamo exhibition on the artist. In the exhibition catalog she noted "the result of grandeur, but at the same time of naturalness" in the *Portrait of a Magistrate* (*Giovan Battista Moroni*, p. 136; Gregori, 1979[1], no. 68, p. 244, both with extensive bibliography). 0

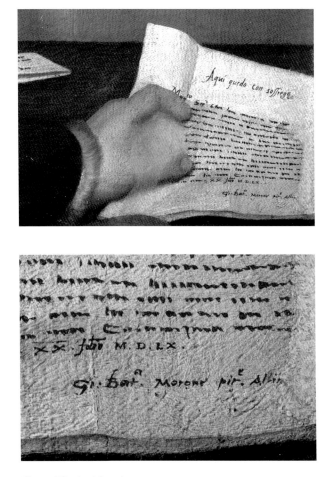

Giovanni Battista Moroni
Portrait of a Man of Letters (The Magistrate)
details

In a recent essay on Moroni's portrait types, Peter Humfrey noted that while the standing pose was usually restricted to artists, soldiers, politicians and nobles, the seated pose was often used to portray doctors, priests or literati: "A key work in the latter category is the *Portrait of a Man of Letters* of 1560 in Brescia. This was apparently the first in a whole series [...] showing black-robed subjects seated in chairs placed at right angles to the picture plane, with their heads turned to face the spectator. The main source of inspiration for the type is likely to have been Titian". Humfrey is here thinking of models like the *Portrait of Ludovico Beccadelli* (Florence, Uffizi), possibly seen by Moroni in Venice on his return from Trento to Bergamo in 1552. But he also mentions earlier precedents like the *Portrait of a Gentleman (The Man with the Blue Sleeve)*, (London, National Gallery) which could be recognized as the prototype "for the over-the-shoulder exchange of glances with the spectator" (Humfrey, 2000[2], p. 32).

Seated on a studded chair with red fringe, the figure is caught in a peaceful moment. He turns toward the observer, who has interrupted his reading of the letter he just opened. A second letter, folded, with only the seal broken, lies on the table covered with a green cloth. The painting clearly shows Moroni's double register, with expertly applied ideas deriving from international state portraits. Mina Gregori likened the general layout of the painting to "similar but more stylized representations in a fixed format by Antonio Mor" (Giovan Battista Moroni, 1979, p. 136), while Humfrey compared the *Magistrate* to Titian's *Ludovico Beccadelli* (2000, p. 32). Moroni portrayed the face of the man without idealization or disguise, presenting him as he was, with the marked bump on his forehead, his thinning hair, and his face muscles beginning to sag. "The somewhat oversized head of the Brescia portrait in relation to the body is characteristic of Moroni's portraiture throughout his career and may be the practical consequence of head and pose having been studied separately" (Humfrey, 2000[2], p. 32).

The magistrate's name could be Ettore, given the clue offered by the heading of the letter. The plain interior is lit by an oblique ray of light suggesting the presence of an open upper window. This light emphasizes the projection of a wall section (on the right) and concentrates attention on the field occupied by the subject. Gregori defined the light background as being "of Brescian derivation" (i.e. after Moretto), pointing out that the bright triangle is here "a direct precedent of Caravaggio's early studies" (*Giovan Battista Moroni*, 1979, p. 136).

The clothes worn by the man give an indication of his office, confirmed by the heading of the letter addressed "Magnifico Segnor" [Illustrious Sir]. His position as a medium–to high-ranking official or magistrate allowed him to wear the ermine-lined cloak and tricorn hat. The latter appears in other portraits by Moroni, such as that of *Canon Terzi* (London, National Gallery) and especially in *Bartolomeo Bonghi* (New York, Metropolitan Museum). A "canon […] but also the rector of Pavia University, a position that allowed the use of the *biretta*, as attested by Cesare Vecellio (*Degli abiti antichi et moderni di diverse parti del mondo*, Venice, 1590, t. 127)" (*Giovan Battista Moroni*, 1979, p. 136).

The motto in Spanish is also fairly common in Moroni's portraits from the end of the 1550s and the early '60s. Through close contacts with people like Isotta Brembati, Gian Gerolano Grumelli (the *Gentleman in Pink*, Bergamo, Moroni collection, dated 1560) and others of their circle, Moroni mixed with the more pro-Spanish Veneto-Bergamo elite and, along with his clients, adopted

Spanish customs. These included the rules of etiquette and behavior introduced by the new European rulers and even the use of Castilian in place of Latin to immortalize the mottoes people adopted for personal prestige. Moroni's relationship with members of the elite is established exclusively by his portraits, their composition and the costumes of their subjects; not by documents, correspondence or contemporary literature, as might be expected in such circles. This is further confirmation of the need for more comprehensive studies of the painter. The maxim written on the letter of the *Magistrate* now in Brescia, "Aquí quedo con sossiego", may be translated as "Here I am at peace (with myself)" emphasizing the dignified composure of the person, content with the position reached. The word "sossiego" that appears here was popular in sixteenth-century Spanish literature. Its meaning of inner peace, quiet and tranquility of spirit described a sentiment that was strongly Humanist and partly religious in nature (thanks to Maria Luisa Cerron Puga for assistance in interpreting this).

The *Portrait of a Man of Letters (The Magistrate)*, dated 1560 and the *Portrait of Bartolomeo Bonghi* in New York are so closely related in type, style and chronology that they must have been painted at more or less the same time, as suggested by Gregori and Humfrey (*Giovan Battista Moroni*, 1979, pp. 288–289; Humfrey, 2000[1], p. 69).

Rossana Sacchi

Lattanzio Gambara

(Brescia 1530–1574)

Apollo

1557
Fresco: 42 1/8 x 71 5/8 in. (107 x 182 cm)
Inv. 91

Ceres

ca. 1557
Fresco: 33 3/8 x 62 3/8 in. (85 x 156 cm)
Inv. 77

Provenance: Brescia, Villa Erba (now Ancelle della Carità convent in San Rocchino), until an unspecified date; Brescia, Pinacoteca Comunale Tosio, from 1875 (Apollo) and 1875 (?,Ceres); Brescia, Santa Giulia.Museo della città, since 1999.
Restoration: 1998, Romeo Seccamani, Brescia.

The two frescoes portray mythological subjects, popular with the Brescian clientele for decorating their houses and *palazzi*. They have usually been considered together because both date from the artist's early career and because the same provenance has been suggested, possibly incorrectly, for both.

Their attribution to Gambara has never been in doubt. He was born in Brescia but first worked with the workshop of the Campi painters in Cremona until 1548. He then returned to Brescia where he began working with Romanino, then employed on his vast fresco cycles, and married his daughter Margherita in 1556. He worked closely with the elderly maestro, who recognized his talent, then continued specializing in frescoes. Few of his vast output of decorative cycles have been conserved. His painting talent and creativity led him to create spectacular, evocative scenes, such that Vasari declared there was no greater painter in Brescia than he (Begni Redona, 1986, pp. 245–247) after his visit in 1566. Gambara is considered the fourth major painter of the Brescian Renaissance after Savoldo, Romanino and Moretto. He absorbed diverse influences and brought these to Brescia, but most of all he popularized the Mannerist style in Brescia. This represented a break from Naturalism that had been partly initiated by Romanino, and was at first marked by great formal elegance before developing into complex, swirling compositions.

The two frescoes belong to the early period, when the influence of Romanino is still evident in the less rigid graphic formulation. But the movement of the bodies is looser and more modulated on the fields of color, and enlivened by the iridescence of the cloth draped across the soft, pink flesh tones. This creates a serenity of atmosphere that is particularly evident in the clear profiles of the divinities.

The nude *Apollo* is stretched out on a soft, iridescent pink cloth that crowns his shoulders; he holds a string instrument in his left hand and a bow at rest in his right. A putto emerges from the right corner holding a flute. The god partly protrudes from a simple, trapezoidal architectural frame, whose form corresponds to the chimney-breast where it was frescoed and from which it was detached at the end of the nineteenth century. Nicodemi (1927, p. 39) said it was bought from the Brescia city council in 1875 (council decision of 14 February 1875); it was exhibited in the Pinacoteca in 1879 (Odorici, 1879, p. 24). Confirmation of its provenance from the Villa Erba on the outskirts of Brescia is documented by Nicoli Cristiani (1807, pp. 48–49). He described the whole cycle seen in a small room on the ground floor of the Erba family's Mompiano residence, which he thought had been painted in 1557. Mercury and Pandora occupied the central vault, under which there was a frieze with Latin mottoes in emblems. Groups of playful children were painted on the parapets of the two windows and Apollo was shown with a cherub above the fireplace. The nine Muses appeared in seven compartments on the side walls. Partly preserved fragments of the frescoes described are still in the villa, as noted by Begni Redona and Vezzoli (1978, pp. 91–92, 224).

In the second panel, Ceres is shown as a young, nude woman with her hair drawn back in affected coquetry and turning her back to the observer. She is leaning on a sheaf

of wheat with her left arm and with the other embracing a cornucopia from which more ears emerge. A putto in front of her bends down a branch to offer her fruit. Here, too, the figure goes beyond the limits of the frame, which in this case is a richly worked frieze with decorative motifs in relief. Although the quality of the fresco is very similar to that of the Apollo (Panazza, Boselli, 1974, pp. 122, 125), it is nevertheless difficult to clearly prove its provenance. If it was originally in the Villa Erba, it would almost certainly have been in another room with divinities representing the seasons or months. The last restoration has returned the freshness of tone and smooth but vigorous brushstrokes to the figure of Ceres. She recalls a similar female figure in the decorative cycle of the Palazzo Lechi in Brescia, where the young Gambara and the elderly Romanino probably worked closely together.

Elena Lucchesi Ragni, Renata Stradiotti

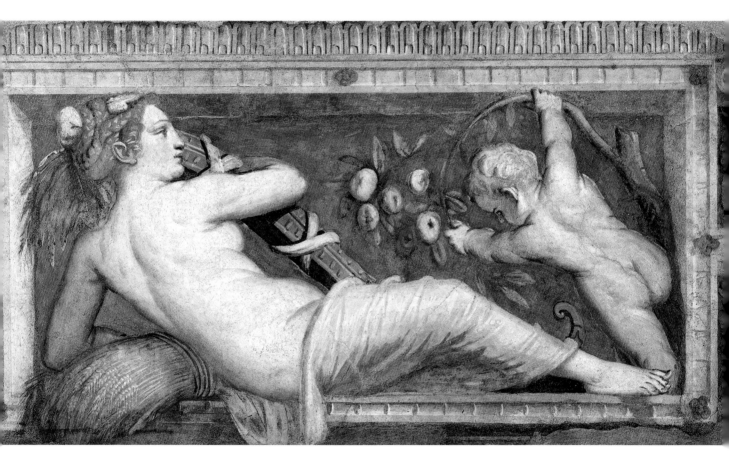

Francesco Paglia

(Brescia 1635–1714)

Earthly Happiness

ca. 1670–75
Oil on canvas; 45 5/8 x 37 3/4 in.
(116 x 96 cm)
Inv. 1048

Eternal Happiness

ca. 1670–75
Oil on canvas; 50 3/4 x 36 5/8 in.
(129 x 93 cm)
Inv. 1049

Lasting Love

ca. 1670–75
Oil on canvas; 46 1/2 x 36 5/8 in.
(118 x 93 cm)
Inv. 1050

Ephemeral Passion

ca. 1670–75
Oil on canvas; 461/2 x 36 5/8 in.
(118 x 93 cm)
Inv. 1051

Provenance: Estate of Teodoro Filippini, 1914; Brescia, Pinacoteca Tosio Martinengo, from 1994.
Restorations: 1964, Giuseppe Simoni, Brescia; 2005, Marchetti & Fontanini, Brescia.

The four paintings were purchased by the City of Brescia from the estate of Teodoro Filippini. They are numbered from 18 to 21 and listed as "eighteenth century Genoa School (?), Four allegoric female figures on canvas, m. 0.93 x 1.8", in the report dated 3 December 1914 made by the then director of the Pinacoteca, Giulio Zappa, illustrating criteria and results from selected works pertaining to the property made available by the bequeather (ASC, Index book XIV, 8/62, II).

The paintings are recorded among the "possessions one hopes to be able to use […] one day […] as simple decorative touches" or "transoms", and were intended to be used to decorate the entrance hall just below the grand staircase of the recently built Loggia.

It was here that Camillo Boselli saw them on 20 January 1954, and precisely numbered them for the first time (numbers which remain intact). In 1990 Elena Lucchesi Ragni retrieved and transported them to the Palazzo Martinengo where they were displayed along the walls of the entrance staircase (AMAS).

The four figures can be attributed to the same series as they are painted by the same hand, and were arranged in pairs. The woman holding flowers in her lap (inv. 1051), for example, corresponds to the woman with the arrow and compass (1050) who faces her and, moreover, the same model is used in both cases. The size of the paintings is the same (118 x 93 cm); but these are not their original sizes. They were probably reduced to fit the splendid eighteenth-century frames in which they remain. The third painting, indisputably attributed to the same hand and portraying a lady with fire and palm branch (1049), measures 129 x 93 cm, i.e., ten centimeters higher than the previous two. This shows that no adaptations were required to make it fit its frame, made in the early 1900s. The fourth frame is also an antique but wider than the others. For this reason it is thought that the fourth painting (1048), whose actual size is 116 x 96 cm, was widened by 3 cm and reduced in height by 13 cm to fit its frame.

The four beautiful ladies personify allegories which can be interpreted based on Cesare Ripa's readings of certain iconographic features: the *Earthly Happiness* (Ripa, 1630, p. 245) is easily recognized in the sensual lady with the jet-black hair portrayed in painting 1048. She seems to be inviting us to share in the comforts of the luxurious palace sat in a park, and is holding out a crown that according to Ripa is the symbol of a "brief and vain happiness". She can also be likened to the ethereal, blond-haired lady of celestial beauty in painting 1049. Here it is not difficult to recognize the "Young nude with golden tresses crowned by laurels

[…] beautiful and resplendent, seated above the starry sky, holding a palm in her left hand and a flame of fire in her right, lifting her eyes upwards in a gesture of gaiety" who according to Perugia iconography symbolizes *Eternal Happiness* (Ripa, 1630, p. 247; this is confirmed by the tiny semi-vanishing stars still distinguishable in the background sky).

Once aware of this contrast between transient and eternal value, it is easy, when approaching the other pair of figures, to discover in the beautiful lady with auburn hair (1051) the *Ephemeral Passion* since according to Ripa, the garland of flowers accompanies a "large, smooth full forehead" (like the emblem of Aristotle) only in the "passion of the spirit devoted to the pleasure that the senses arouse" ["passione d'animo volta al piacere di cosa che le sia portata dal senso"] (Ripa, 1630, p. 81); in this case found in the gift of joy, as fleeting, alas, as cut flowers destined to wither.

She can be juxtaposed with her companion in painting 1050 who displays "a garland of lilies and privet on her head" and who is "white, soft and sound–the most indispensable qualities in a beautiful lady" and who holds in her hand "an arrow that makes a wound at first hardly felt, but which gradually increases in pain, and penetrating deeply, is difficult to remove" ["una ghirlanda di gigli e ligustri in testa", è "bianca, morbida e soda, qualità necessarissima in una donna bella" e reca in mano "un dardo, che fa una piaga nel principio quasi insensibile e poi cresce a poco a poco, e penetrando molto dentro, è difficile potersi cavare"] (Ripa, 1630 p. 28). She cannot but be indicative of beauty inspired by love and, metaphorically, *Lasting Love* (of which the compass suggests "measured moderation" and her hand on her breast "sad devotion"). The use of the same pleasing model with the dimpled chin as the previous painting subtly alludes to the possible transformation of that short-lived passion into this permanent sentiment.

The entire series is inspired by a moralist celebration of the stability and durability of married love and its distinction from the ephemeral passions of the flesh; a series which is easy to associate with the decoration of a noble and austere palace restored to welcome a new bride.

The four allegorical ladies reveal Alessandro Tiarini's simplification of Reni's chilling sentimentality according to the formula practiced by Guercino and by Albani around the year 1655. Crushing the drapery into repeated iridescent folds follows the Parma-Paolo Veronese version of Venetian invention, which was imported to Bologna by Agostino Carracci and became a stylistic feature of the Emilian School. It identifies this as the work of a painter from the ensuing generation trained in such workshops as those of Canuti, Pasinelli and Cignani. The animated pose of the young ladies, signifying their eagerness, seems to resemble the styles of the Emilian born Lanfranco.

The combination of these marked Emilian touches with the general palor of the paintings (perhaps due to a defect in the preparations which caused reddish and leaden colors to emerge), contrasting particularly with the festive tone and the cramped compositional arrangement which makes the figures seem awkward in the space, recall the stylistic characteristics of the work of Francesco Paglia, who had already been identified for some time by Brescian scholars (Stradiotti, 1981). These allegories, constructed according to the painter's particular and exclusive style, refer however to the *genius loci* of the seventeenth century. His workshop dominated the Brescian market in 1670 and continued to thrive for nearly a century, thanks to the involvement of his sons Angelo and Antonio. Furthermore, the allegories actually reveal that portraiture tendency (in the depiction of models) which is always postulated with the support of old sources, but never verified.

Indeed as Pellegrino Orlandi had already stated of Paglia, "scholar of Guercino […], cultured, gallant, well-mannered and virtuoso painter […] produced paintings of good impasto and portraits very alike on a large and small scale" (1704, p. 177), and as Luigi Lanzi wrote of him in 1789, "pupil and a follower of Guercino […] his strength lay in his portraits […] he also created religious panels […] one of the most esteemed of which is in the possession of the Carità (of Brescia). […] He is the author of good impasto and good chiaroscuro, but of little inner spirit and at times his long shapes are overwhelmingly feeble" (1809, III, p. 264). The painter himself claims more than once in his *Giardino della Pittura*–a guide to Brescia in which the works found in the city and its surroundings are described–to be a student of the "Cavalier da Cento".

In unexpected confirmation of the Paglia attribution, the same model used in *Lasting Love* and *Ephemeral Passion* reappears dressed as *Saint Lucy* in the painting belonging to the church of San Quirico di Muscoline and today held by the parish. Michela Valotti attributed this painting to the circle of Paglia, directly linking it to the controlled classicism of the *Sibyl* by Guercino and Domenichino (2004, pp. 37–40).

Francesco Paglia, *St Lucy*
Muscoline (Brescia), parish church

Similarly unexpected is their affinity to the beautiful *Allegorical Figure* (private collection) signed and dated 1673, which Luciano Anelli attributed to Paglia (together with a new companion; Anelli, 1985). Further similarity lies in the yielding receptiveness associated with the noble, dreamy beauty of the model portrayed. This connection is further accentuated by the fact that these *Allegories* must have originated, as Anelli rightly states, "from a group made for an aristocratic household.

"The artist's portraits of young models should also be raised to this level. I hope a good many are conserved in various Brescian noble collections. Unfortunately, I am only able to point out one of the late portraits, as already the dreariness of the artist's communicative abilities were being deadened by his haughty detachment" (Pinacoteca Tosio Martinengo, inv. 1092).

Once further scrutiny concerning the rightful attribution of the *Allegories* is no longer necessary, it would be good to clarify what indications they provide on the important topic of the painter's early work. It is known that his career began with the beautiful altarpiece of *St Francis in Glory surrounded by Saints Rocco, Sebastian and Nicholas of Tolentino* at the Brescia Carità, an altarpiece already praised by Lanzi and signed and dated 1672 (Boselli, 1942–45, p. 93), and with the *Birth of St John the Baptist* at Telgate, dated 1673 (Stradiotti, 1987, p. 248). Those same years saw the appearance of the altarpiece of *St George Victorious over the Dragon*, the *Madonna in Glory* at Cellatica, and *St Anthony of Padua* in Sarezzo (Stradiotti, 1994, pp. 130, 131), in addition to the *Assumption of St John the Evangelist* in Brescia, reasonably dated to 1672–75 and presented by Renata Stradiotti (1981, p. 29). The *Blessed Virgin and Saints*, now at the Brera, which Mariolina Olivari showed was from Santa Chiara in Brescia (1990, p. 4) and which was no doubt painted by 1675, given that it was cited in the first version of Paglia's book *Giardino* completed that same year, and the *Assumption of the Virgin with St Catherine and Lucy* from the church of Santa Maria Assunta in Piano di Bovegno, signed and rightly dated between the years 1675–80 by Renata Stradiotti (1994, pp. 102, 103), are also noteworthy.

These works repeat the extreme physical exaggeration of the *Allegories*, the spatial awkwardness, the Guercino-like chromatic range (the blasts of brick red compared to the deep blues), and even the true stylistic features such as the little rivulets of light that wind through the large folds of drapery or the scorched-brown overtones for which Stefano Fenaroli had already reproached Francesco Paglia in the past, attributing them to the "terra d'ombra" (1877, pp. 193, 194); however they may be more recent.

In other words, the group of paintings seems to be the fruit of the artist's earliest work carried out in his hometown, until now known only by the *Virgin in Glory with Saints Lawrence and Fermo* at Cogozzo, signed, with the indicative date of 1665–70 proposed by Renata Stradiotti (1994, pp. 106, 107).

The fact that Paglia's work for Brescia had been underway for quite some time can be confirmed, even if indirectly, by period sources: Marco Boschini in the *Miniere della Pittura*, published in 1674, indicated how at that time the "worthy painter" passed his time "partly in Brescia, partly in Venice" (p. 50); a letter dated 18 May 1675, sent by Boschini to Cardinal Leopoldo dei Medici, ascertained that in those years he had completed a series of over "sixteen paintings" for the church of San Nicolò on the Lido of Venice (L. Procacci, V. Procacci, 1965, p. 101).

In order for Paglia's work to have been recognized and published by 1674, his activity in Venice must have begun well before that date (Anelli, 1996, p. 336), perhaps even as early as 1666–the year in which Guercino, his maestro, died and the same year in which Paglia's presence in that studio ended. He also conducted other activities in the Brescia area alongside those listed above and must have returned to the Brescia area as early as the 1660s. Proof of this can be found in the fact that the first manuscript of the *Giardino della pittura* was concluded by the year 1675 (ms. Queriniano G. IV. 9, [P2], according to the codification proposed by Boselli). The manuscript was the result of vast research made on the artistic patrimony of Brescia; research which helps ascertain that his activity began many years earlier, probably in response to the publication of the *Carta del Nauegar Pitoresco* (1660) by Boschini and, therefore, very close to the *ante quem* date of 1662, which Boselli himself did not uphold.

Fortunately it is possible to present some pictorial proof parallel to the *Allegories*. The same controlled sentimentality, the luxurious garments with their flowered pattern and bright flashes, the sudden emergence of the protagonist from the shade, recur in the *Martyrdon of St Catherine*, belonging to the Panajotov collection in

Francesco Paglia, *Martyrdom of St Catherine*
Zagabria, Panajotov collection

Francesco Paglia, *Mary Magdalene Renouncing Worldly Goods*
private collection

Zagabria and published by G. Gamulin (1963, p. 64, fig. 9). This is signed "F. PALEA F." and comes from the altar of the suppressed church of the nuns of Santa Maria della Pace in Via Tosio, Brescia (from which it was expropriated in 1808 under Napoleon), as Renata Stradiotti demonstrated (1981, pp. 27, 28). The date of 1675, which has been established by its listing in the first edition of the *Giardino della Pittura*, is too loose and should be narrowed by a few years: the dramatic action centered around the martyr who is already on the platform and exposed to the executioner is too alive and vivid not to be given a date nearer to the versions of the same theme painted by Paolo Veronese, Bernardino Campi, Ludovico Carracci, Alessandro Tiarini and Antonio Carneo. In fact, the *Martyrdon of St Julian* by Carneo, commissioned for the church of San Giuliano in Venice, not only repeats the impending threat of the executioner and the agonizing action of execution, but also the cylindrical shape of the fatal platform encircled by stones (in the *Ricche minere* by Boschini, 1674 shows that the work was already underway).

Mary Magdalene Renouncing Worldly Goods is a work of the same period intended for private devotion and anticipates the *Birth of Saint John the Baptist* at Telgate. The *Magdalen* was formerly on the Bologna art market and I can pubblish it thanks to Angelo Mazza. The saint was arranging her blond hair and adorning it with a charming string of pearls when the vision of Christ in Passion suddenly appeared to her in the mirror, making her aware of her vanity. With a repentant gesture she decides to sacrifice such vanities by detaching herself from all worldly display (an extraordinary development on the theme of the Magdalen in which the mirror is testimony to her repentance and along the same lines as the observations made in the paintings of Francesco Cairo and Georges de La Tour both of whom were, in turn, inspired by Caravaggio). This painting also bears an inscription, perhaps a signature, from the seventeenth century which attributes it to Francesco Paglia, as does its style. It also helps identify it as one of the artist's earliest known works–seeing that it is consistent with the advances of Emilian masters from the same generation, such as Lorenzo Pasinelli and Domenico Maria Canuti–and is a forerunner of developments in the subsequent generation by such artists as Giovanni Antonio Burrini and Gian Gioseffo Del Sole. It can only be by an artist working in the Emilia area, or one who had just come from there.

Prior to this painting, I know only of others that are clearly derived from Guercino. One such, *St Barbara*, had already been attributed to Paglia in the 1800s. I saw it some time ago at a restoration studio in Reggio Emilia (communicated by Angelo Mazza) adorned by lustrous folds that presage the glistening streaks of satin shown in the maestro's later figures.

It is a pity no earlier examples are available to discuss the hypothesis, which Enrico Maria Guzzo (1983) proved to be completely documented, that the side painting of the chapel of Santa Francesca Romana was attributed to Paglia. This painting portrays the *Apparition to the Saint of Her Dead Evangelist Son* located in Santa Maria in Organo in Verona. Its decoration seems to have been concluded by 1658, when the 23 year old Paglia had not yet made his mark within the Guercino workshop.

The new group of paintings here do, however, show the best side of the Brescian Maestro; that to which Giulio Antonio Averoldi alluded when he emphasized with baroque affectation "quanto bon grano sia uscito da questo Paglia" / "How much talent was shown by this Paglia" (1700, p. 94). It brought immediate and early fame to the painter, in addition to subsequent success outside the province in Bergamo, Verona, Trento, Padua and Venice. This success should not be understood as merely based on his extremely extensive and hasty subsequent production but on his reassembling of series of canvases, reused without proportion or aim. Their sparkle from his device of flickering light is not enough to redeem them from routine ordinariness.

All the same, it is very likely that his desire for social affirmation and recognition, obtained through his position as supreme arbiter of aesthetic tastes (the characteristic of a gentleman) and having direct control over his critics by publishing the city's pictorial guide (according to the classic model offered by Vasari and repeated by many others such as Titi, Sandrart, Scaramuccia, Santagostino, Passeri, Ratti), helped distance him from creative activity. It reduced him to a mere hoarder of works. This is documented in the professorial haughtiness–veiled by a professed reserve and passed off as melancholic detachment–of the *Self-portrait* in the Uffizi. It recurs in the pompous subtitle "Ambra de' dilettanti e Calamita dei virtuosi" in the *Guide* which he himself proudly produced and which was the result of thirty years' research. It is even more evident in his prestigious acquiring of the public commission to produce the portraits of the Veneto Provveditori (local Superintendents) of Broletto, an assignment that was to be followed-up by Ceruti (Maccarinelli, 1747 and 1751, ed. Boselli, 1959[2], pp. 47–48).

Paglia's best work is found in his earliest paintings like the group exhibited here. They are few and far between compared to those he executed after he had gained recognition and success. Every future and hoped-for attribution among the numerous portraits proposed should be measured against the charm of the models depicted here, exuberant but restrained by modesty, open yet contained by their own reserve.

Angelo Dalerba

Antonio Rasio

(active from 1677)

Spring, Summer, Autumn, Winter (The Four Seasons)

1685–95
Oil on canvas; 37 3/4 x 55 1/8 in. each (96 x 140 cm)
Inv. 956, 957, 958, 959

Provenance: Verolanuova (Brescia), San Lorenzo parish; Brescia, Pinacoteca Tosio Martinengo, since 1952, by acquisition.
Restoration: 1953, Ottemi Della Rotta, Milan.

The paintings show the four seasons according to a formula established by the Milan painter Giuseppe Arcimboldi (1527–93). But they actually stem from an older tradition of allegories, or anthropomorphic metaphors, widely used in Roman frescoes and mosaics and endorsed by Latin poetry. Indeed, they clearly relate to the definitions given in the second book of Ovid's Metamorphosis, especially in Cesare Ripa's translation of 1593 (1630, III, pp. 96–100), where spring is a maiden, in green skirt, scattering flowers of vermilion and yellow; summer is a lady, whose face glows and whose head is crowned with ears of wheat; autumn is a mature man, with red face and white beard, and wreaths of ripe grapes, figs, chestnuts and acorns; winter is an old man, stiff and trembling, with teeth chattering, covered in ice from head to toe [spring, "una donzella /…/ che verde ha la gonnella, sparta di fior vermigli e gialli"; summer, "una dama il cui viso arde e risplende [e] che di spighe il capo ha cinto"; autumn, "un huomo più che maturo /…/ che il viso ha rosso, e già la barba imbianca /…/ di uve mature son le sue ghirlande /…/ di fichi e ricci di castagne, e ghiande"; winter, "un vecchio, [che] sta rigido, e freme, e batte il dente / e ghiaccio [è] ogni suo pel dal capo al piede"].

In classical antiquity the cycle of the seasons was likened to that of human life. Analogies were made between the irrepressible vitality of spring and childhood, the exuberant strength of summer and youth, the declining fertility of autumn and maturity and the icy rigors of winter and old age. This was further expanded by Galeno and the neo-Platonists, and again in the middle ages by occultists, alchemists, devotees of Paracelsus, interpreters of Nostradamus, cabalists and emblematists, who found arcane symbolic connections between the astonishing variety of the seasons' natural manifestations and their primeval causes.

Spring, summer, autumn and winter were seen as corresponding to four divinities (Venus, Ceres, Bacchus and Vulcan); four elements (air, fire, earth and water); four humors of the body (blood, bile, black bile and phlegm); four temperaments (sanguine, choleric, melancholic and phlegmatic), four ages of man, along with the "virtues, principle sciences, parts of the world, winds, causes of human sciences" (Ripa, 1630, I, p. 209).

Arcimboldi's success at the imperial courts of Maximilian II of Habsburg in Vienna and his son Rudolph II in Prague, still shrouded in the mists of an esoteric, necromantic culture, was certainly due to his ability to give form to these speculations.

The painter did not want to limit the seasons to a mere display of their relative flowers and fruits, but to make them actually consist of these by metaphorical allegory, giving them more profound meaning through mimicry. These ambiguous inventions can be seen both as human figures and vegetal anthologies, thereby tricking our perception of them, which is made to oscillate between two mental interpretations of the same image.

The images only reveal the uncertainty and fallibility of our senses, however. They are certainly unable to alleviate the bewilderment caused by an assumed contact with unfathomable reality. But this is what the instigators of a large part of modern art (Surrealism, Dadaism, Pittura Metafisica and Abstract art) wanted to believe, reviving the fame of Arcimboldi as their precursor and inspiration.

This twentieth-century recovery, which may also explain the purchase of the group for the Pinacoteca, made it quite natural for the first mention of the painting after its acquisition to make reference to Arcimboldi. Camillo Boselli attributed it to "Followers of Arcimboldi" (1953², p. 22), an opinion con-

firmed in the "Arcimboldi-style mannerist" of the same year (1953[1], p. 213).

Benno Geiger (1954, p. 63) then connected the group to the golden name of "Arcimboldi" in person. But he also linked this series to the one, undoubtedly by the same hand, consisting of the *Spring* and *Summer* in the Wadsworth Atheneum in Hartford Connecticut (inv. 1939/212 and 1939/211), and an *Autumn* and *Winter* (untraced). More or less the same size as the Brescian paintings, the first two were bought from the Parisian dealers Renou and Colle by the Atheneum; the second two from the same source by the New York collector Edward James. Gaetano Panazza subsequently agreed with the attribution to Arcimboldi in his catalogs for the Brescia Pinacoteca (1958, p. 40; 1959, p. 57).

In the meantime, a more international critical current had been set off by Francine-Claire Legrand and Félix Sluys. They suggested attributing the Hartford group to a "Fleming working in Italy" under the name of Francesco Zucchi, the brother of the Florentine painter Iacopo, on the slender basis that Baglione had attributed the invention of portraying the seasons as fruit and flowers to him. The suggestion is certainly incorrect, because Zucchi's only known painting, the altarpiece at San Giacomo degli Incurabili in Rome, is quite different from the *Seasons* in many respects. The suggestion that the "background landscapes" in the American paintings are by "a different hand" is equally erroneous: the leaves and fronds are quite similar in both series.

The editor of Selearte (probably Carlo Ludovico Ragghianti) went along with the attribution to Francesco Zucchi in an article on Arcimboldi (1955, p. 31), as did Gaetano Panazza in his book on Brescian museums of 1968 (p. 143). This was also the opinion of Eugenio Battisti in 1989 in the new edition of his *L'antirinascimento* (I, fig. XV, pp. 126 and 127).

After this (quite unfounded) attribution seemed to have gained acceptance, Camillo Boselli (1971, p. 35) found a letter dated Venice 26 May 1592 at the Biblioteca Queriniana in Brescia, in the art archive of the Gambara counts. It was written by their Venetian representative, who stated that he had "paid for the 4 seasons of the year", whose "purchase for 4 scudi" he had previously mentioned.

Boselli enthusiastically connected this to the painting just bought by the Pinacoteca, justifying its incongruous presence in the Verolanuova parish with an earlier provenance from Castel Merlino, the feudal residence of the Gambara counts in Verola. The result was that the paintings acquired an earliest possible date of 1592 and Venetian provenance.

Antonio Rasio, *Spring*
Wadsworth Atheneum Museum
Hartford, Connecticut

Antonio Rasio, *Summer*
Wadsworth Atheneum Museum of Art
Hartford, Connecticut

The discovery thus led back to Arcimboldi and an earlier date. In the Pinacoteca guide written by Bruno Passamani (1988, pp. 82–83) the attribution was changed to "an unknown artist of Archimboldesque genre, around 1592". This identification then became more or less standard in each subsequent citation due to its official authority. It accompanied the paintings at the Colombian Exposition of Seville in 1992, for example, (Gonzáles Bernáldez, p. 47), where an obvious slip converted what was certainly intended as "ca. 1590" into an impossible "ca. 1520".

However, the restricted circulation of Boselli's contribution and the much later publication of the museum guide allowed for other quite different readings in the intervening 20 years.

The "Anonymous Italian of the mid-seventeenth century" suggested by J. Bosquet (1956, p. 16), and Boselli's "effectively from the seventeenth century" (1958, p. 336), converged in Francesco Porzio's brilliant formula: "manner of Arcimboldi-Italian school of seventeenth century" (1979, p. 11). The latter must also be merited with having recognized the decorative function of the Brescian "reclining odalisques".

Adalgisa Lugli expressed much the same opinion in the Biennale di Venezia catalog (1986, p. 121), as did Alessandro Morandotti and Mauro Natale, though with a further decisive slide toward the "Lombard School, eighteenth century" (1989, p. 202, no. 45).

In her entry for the Wadsworth Atheneum of Hartford catalog of 1991 (pp. 268–270), Jean Cadogan described the *Seasons* in that museum as "possibly by another, less skilled hand" than the Brescians, belonging to an "Anonymous Italian of the seventeenth century". She then noted that "the state of the studies does not allow greater precision".

A response to this challenge requires closer scrutiny of the paintings.

Starting from the "objective" information, the vegetable species used in the Brescian paintings are more or less the same as those used by Arcimboldi (particularly in the *Vertumno* of 1591: note the similar use of lettuce to form the sleeves of *Spring's* corset, and cherries for its eyes). But in *Autumn* there is also corn ("evidently more widely distributed in the meantime") for the body and peppers for the nose and clavicles.

These new vegetables had been imported from America. They were introduced to Venice during the sixteenth century and slowly spread through the Po plain, reaching Lombardy only after the plague of 1630.

Furthermore, the sedimentary rock *Summer* is leaning on can only be seen in such complete form in the Alps and their foothills, as can the martagon lily decorating his forehead and the broad-leafs behind it. The cedars of *Winter* are also from this region, but grow only in the Garda area.

Everything combines to indicate a dating much later than 1591–even far into the 1600s–and a Bergamo-Brescia origin.

The physical components of the pictures also concur: the coarse craquelure is at least late-seventeenth century and the curls of the Mannerist scrolls on the frames have begun to unravel into the flowing volutes of Bernini's Baroque.

This style arrived in the Po area via the Farnese court of Parma, and was introduced to the Oglio river area by Fantoni's workshop. The frames could even be an early indication of Andrea Fantoni's art. After an apprenticeship in Parma and Edolo, he returned to his native Rovetta in 1682 to take over his father's workshop, inspiring its increasing success in the Brescia-Bergamo area (Ferri Pittaluga, 1978, pp. 79–81).

The stylistic elements are even more convincing. The four figures have been freed of the iconic rigidity of the sixteenth century and are arranged to entertain us. With philosophical cheerfulness, they offer an impartial dialogue on the transience of human life. The melancholy intoxication of maturity and the disconsolate coldness of age contrast with the joyfulness of childhood and the exuberance of youth.

The female Seasons are no longer restricted to Arcimboldi's half busts but are finally given full form. They recline in relaxed poses, as opposed to the more vigorous postures of the male Seasons.

The entire figures and their accessories are simulated by vegetal components, culminating in the chilly *Winter*. He is protected by a sheepskin edged with a frost of thistle and warms himself at mock embers of turnips and flaming apples.

If the charm of their anthropomorphic presence is momentarily ignored, they are revealed as simple compositions of objects jumbled onto a surface in the typical "showy" arrangement of busy, late seventeenth-century still lifes. Indeed, the thick, "creamy" grain of the chard leaf in *Summer* clearly resembles the broad weave of carpets by Fieravino (Maltese) and Bartolomeo Bettera of Bergamo.

The same suggestion is given by the decorative, anecdotal detail of the little clouds and the plume of smoke in the background of *Winter*: almost an early, eighteenth-century "capriccio".

A decisive clue is then given by the spectacular refraction of the sun between clouds in the landscape backgrounds of the two Hartford canvases, which are certainly by this same artist. They show a direct knowledge of the splendid inventions for which the Dutch painter Pieter Mulier was renowned, known in Italy as Cavalier Tempesta [Sir Storm]. He stayed in Brescia between 1695 (when he met the Milanese landscape artist Carlo Antonio Tavella; Roethlisberger-Bianco, 1970, passim) and 1697, so the American paintings must certainly be related to that period. Mulier was in Milan from 1684. He then crossed the Po plain twice, stopping first in Parma in 1686, then in Venice in 1687–90, before returning to Milan via Brescia and Bergamo in his final years, 1690–1701.

All the objective (botanical, phyto-historical, geological), material (paint and woodwork) and stylistic data (detachment from the arcane symbolic morality of Arcimboldi, allegorical-decorative attitudes, knowledge of the works of Bartolomeo Bettera and Tempesta), definitively sever any link with the 1592 document and its related attributions, and suggest rather an artist working in the Brescia-Bergamo area in the last decades of the seventeenth century.

A closer study within these limits allows the question of attribution to be finally resolved. The same person who painted the Seasons can be recognized–though at an earlier age–in the *Still life* dated "1677" and signed "Antonio Rasio", in the Brescia museum of Santa Giulia (inv. 747). This work came to the civic museums as part of the Ferioli-Mignani legacy.

The idea that it is a less confident and earlier work by the painter of the *Four Seasons* is at first suggested by the repetition of stylistic features: the creamy expanse of carpet resembling the chard leaves, the slightly nervous execution of the flowers and fruit (in a selection that anticipates that of the *Seasons*), and the showy composition, with the objects arranged, this time on the marble lid of the chest, but in the same way as in the allegories.

The composition is also intended to be allegorical-moralizing: the symbols of pleasure (the spinet stands for music, the wine for friendship, the precious coffer for wealth), worldly success (the helmet symbolizes military glory, the globe and books scientific distinction) and gratification of the senses (the flowers and fruit represent fleeting, transient joys) are precariously balanced on a large, precious carpet, so are ready and waiting to be looted by fate. They represent a *Vanitas*, a symbol of the emptiness of earthly goods. One should therefore be ready to abandon these without hesitation or regret, as the bas-relief on the chest also advises. It shows Agamemnon ready to sacrifice his beloved daughter Iphigenia at Diana's command.

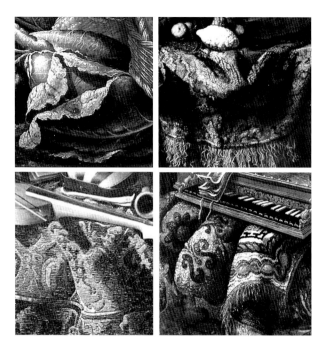

Chard, detail of *Summer*
by Antonio Rasio, Pinacoteca
Tosio Martinengo

Carpet, detail of *Still life* by
Francesco Fieravino
il Maltese, Rivet collection, Paris

Carpet, detail of *Still life*
by Bartolomeo Bettera,
California Palace of the Legion
of Honour, San Francisco

Carpet, detail of *Vanitas*
by Antonio Rasio, Santa Giulia
Museo della città, Brescia

The patron who commissioned the work was probably oblivious to the references to his erotic inclinations. He was presumably the owner of the helmet depicted with Venus crouching on the visor. She is "at the top of his thoughts" and therefore their "predominant passion". Every detail is intentionally infused with meaning.

The painting offers another surprise: the Venus and telamon holding the cabinet-coffer have the same litheness as the Venus-Flora statue in the background of the Hartford Spring. This creates a more direct connection with the more distant of the two groups.

On the basis of these links, the two groups of *Seasons* can certainly be attributed to the painter of the *Vanitas*: the same "Antonio Rasio" who signed and dated "1677" that painting on the musical score (the word "Pieno" is actually part of the real musical notation, indicating that it should "be played by all instruments", providing a cryptic clue as to the symbolic nature of the work).

Dating the Brescia *Seasons* later than the *Vanitas* allows for their more mature development. Their backgrounds already

129

Antonio Rasio, *Vanitas*
Santa Giulia
Museo della città, Brescia

Venere-Flora, detail
of *Spring*
by Antonio Rasio, Wadsworth
Atheneum Museum
Hartford, Connecticut

Telamone, detail of *Vanitas*
by Antonio Rasio Santa Giulia
Museo della città, Brescia

show the influence of Cavalier Tempesta. The Hartford paintings are even more advanced, with figures that are better proportioned and easier to read (the elusive smile of the two Seasons is finally captured, along with the vegetable earrings, bracelets, necklace and the generously low-cut corset). The aerial depth and crystalline brightness of their landscapes, incomparably better than the Brescian ones, suggest a direct knowledge of Cavalier Tempesta and combine to suggest a dating of around 1695–1705.

The subsequent repetition of the *Seasons* as a typical theme, accurately perfected and embellished at every turn, documents the survival of Arcimboldi's ideas in Lombardy even at the end of the seventeenth century, as do some of the series incorrectly attributed to him by Geiger.

The eight paintings making up the *Seasons* here attributed to Antonio Rasio document his work at least until the end of the seventeenth century, giving an initial chronological reference. They can also be used to place the group of other early works attributed to him by Alessandro Morandotti (1989, p. 280).

Some details suggest important contacts between the artist and the Florentine grand ducal court: the Venus wringing her hair may be taken from the Giambologna fountain for the Medici villa in Petraia and the telamon from a design by Cellini for Fontainebleau (now in the Woodner collection).

The desire for a universality of meaning shown by Rasio in the *Vanitas* offers the chance to make some conjectures on the function of the animals in the Brescian *Seasons*. He may have intended the unfolding of the year to be accompanied by parallel events from the animal world. The sheep of *Spring* would thus recall the "saltat pecus" (Horace), alluding to the season when animals are in heat; the two nesting ducks of *Summer* would symbolize the gestation of their fruit; the nocturnal owls of *Autumn* recall the decline of the year toward the darkness of the winter solstice, all according to his own newly created iconography.

The 1592 document certainly relates to other, possibly older, paintings. They may have been replaced (but not repeated) by these ones almost a century later because they were damaged, obsolete or simply unsuitable for a new style of furnishing.

Angelo Dalerba

Pieter Mulier called Cavalier Tempesta

(Haarlem 1637–Milan 1701)

Nocturnal Landscape with Shepherds

1697
Oil on canvas; 51 1/2 x 78 3/4 in. (131 x 200 cm)
Inscription at bottom center, above sleeping dog:
CAVALIER/PIETRO TEMPESTA/ BRESCIA 1697
Inv. 646

Provenance: Brescia, Ferioli Mignani collection, until 1929; Brescia, Pinacoteca Tosio Martinengo, since 1930.
Restorations: 2002 (inv. 646) and 2003 (inv. 645), Romeo Seccamani, Brescia.

In his monograph on Pieter Mulier, Röthlisberger-Bianco (1970, pp. 116, 118, nos. 326, 344) published the two paintings separately. Their provenance from the Ferioli Mignani collection and their similar dimensions and compositional structure, however, suggest they were probably conceived as a pair and they were published as such by Jansen, Meijer, Squellati Brizio (2001–02, II, p. 102, nos. 563–564). They may both also have been originally in the collection of the noble Malvezzi family of Brescia. This is indicated by the inscription on the back of the *Landscape with Shepherdesses and Hunting Scene* and the words "Eredità conte Federico" [Count Federico legacy] in eighteenth-century writing on the label previously on the back of the *Nocturnal Landscape with Shepherds* (Brescia, AMAS, Archivio dei Musei d'arte e Storia).

The two paintings were previously thought to be from Pieter Mulier's studio (Panazza, 1959, p. 71; Passamani, 1964, p. 620), but recent restorations have confirmed their excellent quality and rightful place among Mulier's own work.

After initial training with his father in his native Haarlem and a brief stay in Antwerp, Mulier went to Italy where he remained for the rest of his life. He spent the second half of the 1650s in Rome, then went to Genoa where he was charged in 1676 with killing his wife and condemned to 20 years' prison. He was eventually freed in 1684 on the condition he leave the city, thanks to the intervention of Vitaliano Borromeo who Mulier had met in Rome. The artist then lived in various parts of northern

Landscape with Shepherdesses and Hunting Scene

1697
Oil on canvas; 51 1/8 x 78 1/4 in. (130 x 199 cm)
Inscription on two wooden slats attached to the new frame (parts of a previous frame?): *B.I.F.; Ill.mo Sig.r Malnezzo n° 2.*
Inv. 645

Italy: Milan in 1684, Parma and Venice in 1687, Venice again from 1688 to 1690, then Vicenza. He returned to Milan and made several visits of varying length to the Bergamo and Brescia areas (Roethlisberger-Bianco, 1970, pp. 18–19 and Rigoni, 1997, p. 146), where his paintings are documented in a number of collections. Early guides mention those of the Fenaroli, (Sala, 1834, p. 120), Duranti (Paglia, 1675–1714, ed. Boselli, 1967, p. 121), Barbisoni, Avogadro, Lechi and Ugoni (Roethlisberger-Bianco, 1970, pp. 137–138) in Brescia.

The artist's repertoire of sea storms (giving rise to his nickname "Cavalier Tempesta" [Sir Storm]), pastoral scenes, coastal views and landscapes with religious and mythological themes made him one of the most popular painters among the nobility in the last decades of the seventeenth century.

His work clearly shows his incorporation of the Netherlandish approach to landscape with the classical influence of Poussin, Lorrain and Claude. There are also references to the more restless, dramatic views of Salvatore Rosa, and to Veneto (Bassano) and Genoa (Castiglione) painting in the figurative elements. These two works are a fine example of how Mulier brought various motifs together in his own personal style. They are part of the group considered by Roethlisberger-Bianco (1970) as representative of the artist's "grand manner": that of the classically inspired pastoral landscape from his late career. In both works he followed a clearly defined pattern of parallel planes, with large trees providing wings around people and animals in the foreground. He then varied the figurative elements and light within this layout, suggesting a moonlit evening atmosphere in the *Nocturnal Landscape with Shepherds* and twilight in the *Landscape with Shepherdesses and Hunting Scene*.

Pieter Mulier called Cavalier Tempesta
Nocturnal Landscape with Shepherds, detail

The first of these shows two shepherds and a flock resting, with some fishermen further back on a riverbank hauling in their nets. A swath of light brightens the dusky atmosphere and is reflected on the water from behind the crown of the trees. The work corresponds iconographically to the artist's various versions of the *Annunciation to the Shepherds* (see the paintings in the private Milan collection, in the Congrega Apostolica of Brescia, the Borromeo collection of Isola Bella; Röthlisberger-Bianco, 1970, p. 124, no. 382; p. 115, no. 316; p. 116, no. 323) several of which feature a sleeping shepherdess. The suggestion that this pastoral scene contains a Biblical reference (Luke 2, 8–9) seems unlikely, considering the lack of any relationship to this in its pendant.

Mulier's various influences are evident in his *Nocturnal Landscape with Shepherds*, particularly those of Bassano and Castiglione in the pastoral motif and animal genre. The dog in the foreground was a model frequently used by the artist in his later years, for example in his *Landscape with Sheep and Goats* in the Staatsgalerie di Stoccarda (Röthlisberger-Bianco, 1970, p. 115, no. 314). A similar version of the scene with fishermen bringing in their nets, though moved to the foreground, can be seen in the *Night View of Arcugnago* (Vicenza, conte Giuseppe Canera di Salasco collection; Röthlisberger-Bianco, 1970, p. 114, no. 307). This was also a typical motif in eighteenth-century Roman landscape, such as in Domenichino's *The Flight into Egypt* in the Louvre (*L'ideale classico*, 1962, fig. 34) and Rosa's *Landscape with Bathers* in the Yale University Art Gallery (Salerno, 1963, fig. 48a). The composition, the type of figure and the arrangement of the flock are very similar to other works by Mulier from the same period, such as the *Pastoral Landscape with Flight into Egypt* of 1696 in Geneva (Musée d'Art et d'Histoire; Roethlisberger-Bianco, 1970, p. 116, no. 322); the dusky atmosphere, the chiaroscuro effects and the ratio of scale between figures and space resemble those of the *Pastoral Landscape* in a private Genoese collection, dated 1701 (Roethlisberger-Bianco, 1970, p. 114, no. 304). There are also more obvious Netherlandish motifs, such as the rustic buildings in the left background, recalling Haarlem landscape painters like Nicolaes Berchem (1620–83) and Pieter Molijn (1595–1661).

The companion painting with lively hunting scene, the *Landscape with Shepherdesses and Hunting Scene*, is almost unique in the artist's work. It follows the Flemish tradition of Paul Bril (1554–1626) and recalls Antonio Tempesta (1555–1630), a Florentine artist who trained with Jan van der Straet of Flanders and worked closely with Bril himself in Rome. Bril's work includes similar hunting scenes, such as those in the Galleria di Palazzo Pitti in Florence (Salerno, 1977–80, I, p. 17, figs. 2.2, 2.3). Many of Antonio Tempesta's landscapes feature hunters on horseback, sometimes with a lady, as in this painting, along with dogs, deer (or other animals) running zigzag through a forest (*The Illustrated Bartsch*, 1984, 37, figs. 1161–63; 1168–69). Signs of Mulier's Dutch and Flemish background are evident in the painting, but the *Landscape with Shepherdesses and Hunting Scene* also has more obvious classical influences dating from his years in Rome, particularly in the bucolic note of the two shepherdesses in the foreground. They recall the paintings of Claude Lorrain, such as the *Landscape with Figures Dancing* (1648–49) in the Galleria Doria Pamphilj in Rome or the *Pastoral Landscape* (1648) in the Yale University Art Gallery in New Haven (Roethlisberger, 1961, II, figg. 197, 204). The smooth definition and typology of the figures, however, suggest that these are not by Mulier himself but by some unidentified assistant.

The composition of the two Brescian paintings, like the rest of Mulier's work, especially from his late career, is influenced by the Roman landscape painting of Poussin, Lorrain and Dughet. However, the Dutch artist made a more vibrant interpretation of their rational, peaceful compositions, with livelier movement in the clouds, a sharper contrast of light and shade and a distinctive naturalism.

Raffaella Colace

Antonio Cifrondi

(Clusone, Bergamo 1657–Brescia 1730)

Seamstress

ca. 1722–1730
Oil on canvas; 46 1/2 x 35 3/8 in. (118 x 90 cm)
Inv. 631

Young Miller

ca. 1722–1730
Oil on canvas; 39 3/8 x 31 1/2 in. (100 x 80 cm)
Inv. 628

Provenance: Brescia, Vitale-Bondini collection, until 1935; Brescia, Pinacoteca Tosio Martinengo, since 1935.
Restoration: 1977, Scalvini & Casella, Brescia.

The two paintings were sold in 1935 to the Pinacoteca by the Vitale-Bondini family of Brescia, along with two other paintings by Cifrondi, an *Old Man Leaning on a Stick* and an *Old Woman with Stick*, still in the Pinacoteca Tosio Martinengo (Dal Poggetto, 1982, p. 485, no. 78). Although the four works are of different sizes, they were probably part of a single group painted to decorate a Brescian residence.

Both the *Young Miller* and the *Seamstress* (of which there are three signed copies: Dal Poggetto, 1982, p. 607, figg. 3, 4, 5) were attributed to Cifrondi by Emma Calabi (*La pittura a Brescia…*, 1935, p. 96), since confirmed in subsequent literature. Cifrondi's clearly recognizable personal technique is apparent in the fluent brushwork and elongated line of the two works, dispelling any doubts as to their attribution. This is further confirmed by the similarity of the two, slightly doll-like figures to Cifrondi's usual repertoire.

The young seamstress is sitting near a window holding a needle and thread in her slightly raised right hand and concentrating on the strip of material she is sewing. The careful study of her action is matched by the precise definition of her modest, dignified clothing, hair style and sewing tools. The dark shape of a hen is rather ambiguously placed in the foreground. Comparison with the surviving copies of the painting, however, show that the bird was on a bench, which was lost in this example when the canvas was cut down at the bottom.

The image of a woman sewing appeared quite frequently in seventeenth- and eighteenth-century genre paintings, by such artists as Michael Sweerts, Monsù Bernardo and Todeschini. Seamstresses were often depicted in a group interpreted as a sewing school, giving the subject an educational theme.

The iconography of the *Young Miller* used by Cifrondi is considerably less common. This is a very rare example of that specific subject, but may be seen as part of the interest in portraying the trades of farmers, craftsmen and the lower classes in general that typified genre painting. Cifrondi produced a very original work in this context, marked by the silent amazement, almost awe with which the miller, seen in profile, gazes at the sheaf of wheat he is holding.

Both paintings are among the finest examples of the painter's large body of work. Their lyrical, thoughtful expressiveness, of great poetic charm, sets them apart from the grotesque, caricature style that often marked Cifrondi's genre painting. This is partly achieved by the chromatic register of the two paintings, entirely played out on pale shades of brown and on milky layers that give the two figures a diaphanous, almost ethereal quality, particularly noticeable in the *Young Miller*: "enchanting, frank", almost a "Pierrot lunaire" (Longhi, 1953, p. XI).

The paintings were probably painted for a Brescian client, helping confirm their probable dating to Cifrondi's stay in Brescia, as pointed out by Dal Poggetto (1982, pp. 484–485, nos. 77, 79). He moved to the city in 1722 and remained there until his death in 1730. The works would therefore date from the same period that Giacomo Ceruti was painting his first genre scenes, also in Brescia, most notably the "Padernello Cycle".

Francesco Frangi

Giacomo Ceruti called Pitocchetto

(Milan 1698–1767)

The Shoemakers

ca. 1725–30
Oil on canvas; 67 3/4 x 76 3/4 in. (172 x 195 cm)
inv. 1774

Provenance: Brescia (?), Avogadro collection, until 1800; Brescia, Fenaroli collection, from 1800 to 1882; Padernello (Brescia), Salvadego collection, from 1882; Brescia, Pinacoteca Tosio Martinengo, since 1997.

The painting was purchased by the Pinacoteca Tosio Martinengo from the Salvadego heirs in 1997 and is in good condition. It appears among those recorded in 1931 by Delogu in Padernello castle (1931, p. 208), so coincides with Ceruti's famous series of genre scenes. This was probably painted for the Brescian Avogadro family, from whom it went to the Fenaroli at the beginning of the nineteenth century. It was then sold in 1882 to the Salvadego family, who hung the works in their castle in southern Brescia (a more comprehensive consideration of the cycle, its collection history and composition can be found on pages 39–47 of this catalog; it must be noted that this painting is not mentioned in the incomplete eighteenth- and nineteenth-century documentation on works painted for the Avogadro).

The painting has been unquestionably attributed to Ceruti and featured prominently in Giovanni Testori's distinguished essay *Giacomo Ceruti. Lingua e dialetto nella tradizione bresciana* (1966, p. XVIII). In order to visually highlight the continuity of the Brescian preference for reality, he compared a detail of the leg resting on the ground of the person on the left with a similar detail in the *Nativity* painted in 1540 by Giovanni Gerolamo Savoldo for the church of San Giobbe in Venice. Gregori saw the painting as "the most advanced and radical elaboration of Ceruti's realism" (1982, p. 435, no. 61) and seemed to favor a date in a middle stage of the "Padernello Cycle", correctly placed by this scholar to his long early period in Brescia (ca. 1720–ca. 1734).

Two shoemakers are at work beside a small, rickety table on which there are various tools of their trade, pieces of wood and leather. A third person on the left is trying on another pair of apparently newly made shoes. The most probable explanation is that this is a client, but his fairly tattered clothing suggests that he, too, may be a craftsman in the same improvised workshop. A length of leather lies on the floor in the foreground of the scene set between the dark walls of a room. It is viewed from slightly above, as in other examples of the "Padernello Cycle", probably to compensate for its viewing from below.

Like most of the other paintings in the series, the theme does not differ from the usual repertoire of earlier genre paintings. The subject of shoemakers at work had already appeared in the works painted in Rome in the mid-seventeenth century by the so-called Bamboccianti (see Terzaghi, 1998, pp. 434–435, no. 107). In a context closer to Ceruti, the subject had been interpreted both by the Clusone artist Antonio Cifrondi and the Austrian painter Giacomo Francesco Cipper, called Todeschini. Cifrondi interpreted the subject as a caricature in the *Cobbler* (Gardone Riviera, Vittoriale) from his Brescian period (ca. 1722–30); Todeschini treated the subject several times, achieving a convincing, acute realism in his *Shoemaker and Woman Sewing*, shown at the important exhibition of genre scenes in Brescia in 1998 (Gruber, 1998, pp. 427–428, no. 96). In that painting, dating from the first decade of the eighteenth century, the craftsman is shown before a work table crammed with tools, pieces of wood and leather. Everything is carefully described and is very similar to the center of Ceruti's painting. But some just completed peasant shoes are also shown in the foreground and background, attesting to a similar interest in reality. Despite the poetic and expressive differences between the stereotyped and smiling inventions of Todeschini and the earnest depictions of Ceruti, a comparison between these similar subjects suggests Todeschini's role as a source of inspiration for Ceruti, at least in terms of theme and iconography. During his long stay in Milan (from 1696 till his death in 1736), Todeschini painted an enormous number of everyday genre scenes with life-size figures for city and rural clients. These often made up whole cycles similar to Ceruti's Avogadro group, such as his six big paintings for the Montesolaro (Como) residence of Count Alfonso Vismara (Proni, 1994, pp. 92–100), probably painted during the second decade of the eighteenth century. Ceruti must have had the opportunity to inspect that considerable production when studying in Milan. It shows a surprising variety of theme, and meticulous description of the smallest detail related to the various scenes: tools, food, cooking utensils, crude pieces of domestic furniture and various forms of simple clothing. Todeschini's work offered an endless exploration of the world and habits of the lower classes, which Ceruti certainly absorbed before portraying his own world of the humble and the outcast with quite a different spirit and intention.

Francesco Frangi

Giacomo Ceruti called Pitocchetto

(Milan 1698–1767)

The Spinner

1730–ca. 1734
Oil on canvas: 50 3/4 x 57 1/2 in. (129 x 146 cm)
Inv. 1961

Provenance: Brescia (?), Avogadro collection, until 1800; Brescia, Fenaroli collection, from 1800 to 1882; Padernello (Brescia), Salvadego collection, from 1882; Milan, Finarte, until 2003; Brescia, Pinacoteca Tosio Martinengo, since 2003 (on deposit from the Hopa company).

The painting came to the Pinacoteca Tosio Martinengo in 2003 on deposit from the Hopa company and is in good condition.

It almost certainly corresponds to the so-called "Padernello Cycle", so was probably painted for the Avogadro family, from where it went to the Fenaroli and then the Salvadego families (a more comprehensive consideration of the cycle, its collection history and composition can be found on pages 39–47 of this catalog). The painting was not listed among those in the Salvadego castle at Padernello by Delogu in 1931, but its place within that series has recently been shown by Carlo Zani (1998, pp. 431). He traced a mention of the painting in papers relating to the will of Filippo Salvadego, owner of the "Padernello Cycle" at the time of its discovery. Prior to this, however, Gregori had already proposed attaching it to that cycle on the basis of its provenance from the Salvadego family.

The painting was noted by Vitale Bloch (1935, p. 14) shortly after Delogu's publication of most of the other paintings in the series, and then universally confirmed as a work by Ceruti. Gregori (1982) convincingly proposed placing it among the last of those painted for the Avogadro group, mainly produced during the artist's youthful stay in Brescia (ca.1720–ca. 1734), on the basis of its refined brushwork.

The sole figure is that of a young spinner seated on a rock in an open, fairly anonymous setting. She is dressed in poor clothes with torn sleeves and is holding a wool winder under her left arm and a spindle between her hands.

The image of the spinner is undoubtedly one of the most common in genre painting. Although this may relate to the iconography of the three Fates (Lachesis and Clotho in particular, being usually assigned to spinning), the great popularity of the subject was more closely associated with amorous and erotic connotations. The inevitably young, winking spinner in some of the works painted between the end of the seventeenth century and the first decades of the eighteenth by Antonio Cifrondi and Todeschini (see Frangi, 1998, pp. 52–53) is at times flanked by a piper, helping to make the vulgar allusions more explicit. Such allusions can also be seen in the interpretations of that same motif around the mid-eighteenth century by Pietro Longhi, particularly in the two versions in the Pinacoteca Querini Stampalia in Venice, whose multiple erotic inferences were the subject of a recent clearly thought out study (Gruber, 1998, p. 440, nos. 118–119; on the popularity of the spinner subject, see also Terzaghi, 1998[2], pp. 437–438, no. 112).

Such examples serve to widen the gap between Ceruti and the normal customs of contemporary Lombard-Veneto genre painting. In Ceruti's austere spinner, all the typical jesting or scurrilous implications of the theme have been sensationally cast aside to leave room for a new, realistically "purified" interpretation. The figure is no longer a vehicle for other meanings, but is given her own authentic, dignified presence, bringing to the scene nothing more than herself, her own normal clothing and her own menial work. The removal of all narrative or anecdotal elements and the openness of the painting and the young woman's pose allow her to recover a silent, almost solemn seriousness. To find comparable commitment and nobility in the

interpretation of genre subjects one must look to the Le Nain brothers and Michael Sweerts, who also painted memorable scenes with spinners that convey a similar human and poetic intensity (Jansen, in Michael Sweerts, 2002, pp. 71–73). The reference to these "fathers" of seventeenth-century pauper painting does not detract from the surprisingly topical nature of Ceruti's works. This is particularly evident in the fluent brushwork and broad painted backgrounds of the canvases in the "Padernello Cycle", now seen as typically eighteenth-century. Despite his quick, cursive drafting, Ceruti achieved a genuinely surprising realism that is admirably illustrated by this painting.

Francesco Frangi

Giacomo Ceruti called Pitocchetto

(Milan 1698–1767)

Two Beggars

1730–ca. 1734
Oil on canvas: 53 x 68 in. (134.5 x 173 cm)
Inv. 550

Provenance: Brescia, Brognoli collection, before 1820, until 1927–35; Brescia, Pinacoteca Tosio Martinengo, since 1927–35. Restoration: 1986, Romeo Seccamani, Brescia.

The painting is in good condition overall; a sizeable pentimento can be seen on the young man's left arm. It is recorded in the collection of the Brescian scholar Paolo Brognoli (Brescia 1763–1835), and was donated to the Pinacoteca by his descendants between 1927 and 1935. His own handwritten catalog from between 1820 and 1823 lists a work at number 386 as "Two beggars, by Ceruti, L.50" (Guerrini, 1927, p. 238). This can certainly be identified as the painting under consideration, as Marini was first to note (1968, pp. 44–45). He also suggested (1966, p. 39; 1968, pp. 44–45) equating it to the "Two beggars by Ceruti" mentioned by Carboni (1760, p. 174) in the collection of the Barbisoni family of Brescia in order to identify its earlier history. But this is not supported by Carboni's excessively generic description.

However, Brognoli certainly did not inherit the painting now in the Pinacoteca, as shown by its noted cost of 50 lire. Moreover, the collection catalog and purchase notes (Guerrini, 1927, pp. 195–256) show that this large collection was personally assembled by Brognoli. He regarded it as complementary to his scholarly pursuits and love of artistic matters and "local heritage". The latter is evident in his role in establishing the Ateneo di Scienze, Lettere e Arti di Brescia, and in publishing a *New Guide to Brescia* in 1826, aimed at recording the artistic heritage in the city after the changes wrought by Napoleon. Brognoli's collection was made up of early and current works (like that of his contemporary Paolo Tosio), bought in various parts of Italy. It was one of the most important assembled in Brescia between the eighteenth and nineteenth centuries so will hopefully in future be given serious recognition allowing at least some of the works mentioned in his catalog to be identified. An indication of its importance is provided by the presence among its hundreds of paintings of a *St Jerome* by Lorenzo Lotto, signed and dated 1515, which can be identified as the painting now in Allentown.

The *Two Beggars* was presented at the exhibition on *La pittura a Brescia nel Seicento e nel Settecento* by Calabi as a work by Ceruti (1935, p. XXXIII, no. 114), since confirmed in subsequent literature. This has often emphasized the intensely dramatic, almost brutal nature of the picture, such as in the exhibition catalog *I pittori della realtà in Lombardia* (1953, p. 73, no. 148), where it is significantly presented under the title *The Two Rogues*.

In the context of an overall review of Ceruti's career (1982, pp. 440–441, no. 83), Gregori suggested dating the work to the first half of the 1730s, or towards the end of his early stay in Brescia.

The painting shows two barefooted men seated outside with only a brick wall as background and a stool in the middle, on which there is a jug, a deck of cards and a screwed up piece of paper. The man on the left, seated on a wooden chair with a straw seat, is holding a cat and wearing an overcoat and big, tattered, military-style hat, suggesting he may be a war veteran fallen on hard times (Terzaghi, 1998[1], p. 350); his partner on the right is seated on a rock and wearing dark trousers and a torn shirt, open at the front, and a straw hat. His right arm is unnaturally bent at the wrist, due to a deformity. The movement of his left arm seems to indicate that he is about to take some snuff, probably taken from the twist of paper on the table.

The motif of a man, usually a tramp, taking snuff

appears quite frequently in genre scenes, often as an allegory for the sense of smell (explicitly seen in the engraving by Giovanni Maria Mitelli, *Li cinque sentimenti alla moda*, of 1710; see *Immagini del sentire*, 1996, pp. 178–179). This is even more evident in the caricature interpretation of the *Old Man Taking Snuff* by Antonio Cifrondi of Clusone, in a private collection (Dal Poggetto, 1982, p. 489, no. 92), probably dating from the end of the painter's stay in Brescia (ca. 1722–30).

The deck of cards was also widely used from the sixteenth century in episodes from everyday life, often associated with soldiers. Ceruti took up the same theme not only in this painting but in two others specifically portraying *Soldiers Playing Cards* (Gregori, 1982, p. 431, nos. 44–45).

Ceruti here conforms to the iconographic tradition of genre scenes, as in most of his pauper paintings. But he presents a quite personal version in which all comic and anecdotal inferences have been removed, along with the allegorical elements still fairly common at the time in genre painting. These were replaced by a total commitment to realism, particularly evident in the magnificent, partly chiaroscuro overcoat of the tramp on the left, and in the poignant, almost portrait-like study of the two faces. The hairy face of the veteran contrasts with the indignant, almost angry face of the young man beside him. These realistic aspects help accentuate the dramatic nature of the painting, which Gregori (1982, pp. 440–441, no. 83) defined as "one of the most intense examples of Ceruti's ability to capture the reality of human misery and the simplest values of life". Her opinion is fully supported by the silent sense of waiting that pervades the scene and the two characters' sharp look toward the observer, similar to many figures in the "Padernello Cycle" paintings.

The *Soldiers Playing Cards* relates to the *Two Beggars* not only by its expressiveness but also by its detail and layout, such as the broad, solemn span of the composition and details like the rock on which the tramp on the right is sitting. This is painted with the same fluent, abbreviated brushstroke seen in many examples in the Padernello group.

The painting can therefore also be dated to the Milanese painter's early stay in Brescia. As suggested by Gregori, he must have painted it towards the end of that period, around the middle of the 1730s. It must finally be noted that the painting has some details that are beneath Ceruti's normal standard, such as the cat and the chair, raising the still unexplored question of the painter's workshop.

Francesco Frangi

Painters' Profiles

Girolamo Romani, called Romanino
(Brescia 1484/87–1560)

Romanino studied in Venice where he had contacts with Giorgione and Giovanni Bellini. His expressive development of Venetian tonalism shows the influence of the Bergamo artist Lotto as well as artists from the North of Europe. He explored this early in his career in the decoration of the Cremona cathedral with his imaginative exploration of a narrative theme, *The Stories of Christ* (1519–1520). Returning to Brescia, he was one of the main exponents, along with Moretto, of the Lombard Renaissance in terms of luminist power and naturalism. This is evident in the altarpieces, such as the *Nativity*, in which he reworked Savoldo's luminist innovations, and took up the compositional and stylistic elements of Giorgione and Titian's painting. Alongside his church commissions, Romanino also produced numerous devotional works for private clients and frescoed decorations of secular subjects for *palazzi* (grand private residences).

Alessandro Bonvicino, called Moretto da Brescia
(Brescia ca.1498–1554)

Along with Romanino, Moretto is considered one of the outstanding figures of the Brescian School. Although he trained in a Venetian environment, his work remained firmly rooted in the Lombard tradition and the realism of Vincenzo Foppa. He lived and worked in Brescia, apart from occasional commissions that took him to Bergamo, Milan and the Veneto area. He was able to interpret his clients' wishes with works of a clear doctrinal commitment, but at the same time introducing everyday reality into the religious subjects, such as in his *Supper at Emmaus*. His emotional dramatic expressiveness increased in the years after 1540. Color often fades into precious grey monochromes, as in the *Ecce Homo and the Angel* (1550), where the relationship between devotional content and formal character is evident, and where his communicative power is emphasized by the expressive use of chromatic dissonances he had learned from Foppa.

Giacomo Ceruti, called Pitocchetto
(Milan 1698–1767)

There is little information on the life of this artist, whose name appears for the first time in 1724 on the back of the *Portrait of Count Giovanni Maria Fenaroli*. He is known to have been commissioned to paint 15 historic portraits of Venetian nobles in 1729. In 1736 he worked in Venice, then in Padua and Piacenza. He was linked to the sixteenth-century figurative tradition and influenced by genre painting of the Northern European tradition, particularly in the incisive drafting and deft characterization of individual types in his early work. He is now mainly known for the works comprising the "Padernello Cycle", considered the high point of his career. These paintings show scenes of daily life populated by beggars and humble craftsmen, which Ceruti presented in all the simple reality of their condition. Ceruti's characters are therefore not the generic types used to enliven genre scenes, but real people; they are poor people with sad, weary expressions that reveal the artist's great commitment to portraying reality.

Giovanni Gerolamo Savoldo
(Brescia ca.1480/85–? after 1548)

Attribution of his early works (*Blessing of Jacob, Hagar and the Angel*) is controversial. They may relate to a period the artist spent in Florence around 1508, given their obvious Florentine and Veneto influences. Venetian tonalism is evident alongside the solid naturalism of the figure. Numerous elements derive from Fleming painting, such as in imaginative and evocative sections of landscape. There are also references to the lesson of Giorgione and Titian. Everything is interpreted in Lombard style: with the subdued colors and dim light that are so typical of some of his "night scenes", such as the *Adoration of the Shepherds* (1540) in the Pinacoteca Tosio Martinengo.

Giovanni Battista Moroni

(Albino, Bergamo
ca. 1520–Bergamo 1579)

Moroni was one of the great masters of the psychological portrait, expressing the individualism of his middle class subjects with unique sensitivity. Apart from his training with Moretto in Brescia, he worked mainly in Bergamo. His oeuvre encompasses religious subjects (*Assumption, Virgin in Glory*), which recall Moretto and the Veneto and German masters, as well as portraiture (*The Unknown Poet, Portrait of a Magistrate*), but it is the portraits that are the basis of his reputation as an illustrious predecessor to Caravaggio. Moroni skillfully combined attention to detail with Venetian influences.

Lattanzio Gambara

(Brescia, 1530–1574)

Gambara was mainly known in Brescia for his fresco decorations. His fanciful and richly creative talent is evident in complex works depicting subjects from the Bible or ancient history. He enriched and transformed the influence of Romanino into a monumental style of great decorative and spatial effect. His fresco work in Brescia shows his mastery in the use of light and color, and his ability to move away from the religious and moral sentiment that typified the work of Moretto and Romanino.

Antonio Rasio

(active from 1677)

Little is known of this artist to whom an important cycle of works in the Pinacoteca Tosio Martinengo, the Four Seasons, was only recently attributed. The group of paintings dating from 1685–95 shows that the painter was active in Brescia at least until the end of the seventeenth century, and thus provides some chronological points of reference. He did not restrict himself to imitation of the compositions of Arcimboldo (who also painted a *Four Seasons,* in 1572): despite some similarities, Rasio showed a detachment from the symbolic morality of the latter. He moved rather towards allegorical decorations that show the influence of the Dutch painter Pieter Mulier, who worked in the Brescia–Bergamo area in the last decades of the seventeenth century. The individual images in the *Four Seasons* fancifully combine the products typical of each season with evocative landscapes that show obvious references to northern styles.

Pieter Mulier

(Haarlem 1637–Milan 1701)

After an initial training with his father in his native Haarlem and a brief stay in Antwerp, Mulier went to Italy where he remained for the rest of his life. He lived in Rome and Genoa, and from 1684 his presence is documented in several cities of the north: Milan, Parma, Venice, Vicenza, Bergamo and Brescia.
His preferred subject of sea storms (giving rise to his Italian name of "Cavalier Tempesta" [Sir Storm]), along with pastoral scenes, coastal views and landscapes with mythological scenes, made him one of the most popular painters among the nobility in the last decades of the seventeenth century. His *Nocturnal Landescape with Shepherds* (1697) and *Landscape with Shepherdesses and Hunting Scene* in the Pinacoteca Tosio Martinengo exemplify Mulier's incorporation of the Netherlandish approach to landscape with the classical influence of Poussin and Claude.

Antonio Cifrondi

(Clusone, Bergamo, 1657–Brescia 1730)

Cifrondi studied in Bologna with Franceschini and traveled to Turin, Grenoble and Paris where he was appointed painter to the duc d'Harcourt. He returned to Bologna in 1689 and moved to Brescia in 1722. Although he only settled in Brescia at the end of his career he had a profound influence on the evolution of figurative art in the city and most especially on the work of Giacomo Antonio Ceruti. His contributions can be seen in the *Young Miller* and the *Seamstress* both of which go beyond the convention of genre figures as metaphors (here the senses of touch and smell) to become autonomous expressions of reality.

Francesco Paglia

(Brescia 1635–1714)

Paglia studied in Bologna with Guercino, He is credited with helping to free Brescian painting of seventeenth-century Mannerism and direct it towards the innovations of the eighteenth century. Aware that he was living in a period of significant changes in art, Paglia wrote a guide to the paintings of Brescia and its district (*Giardino della pittura*) which appeared in several editions. It contained considerations of an aesthetic and moral nature on artists and their works. Paglia's own paintings can be seen in the churches of San Giovanni and San Francesco in Brescia. His classically modeled forms show how he looked to tradition for the basis of a pictorial language that combined the beautiful, the natural and the practical.

Luca Mombello
(Orzivecchi 1518–after 1588)

Mombello started work in Moretto's workshop carving frames, but quickly became one of his more stalwart followers. He sought to carry on Moretto's style in form and composition. His painting, however, is distinguished by a marked decorative tendency. He enriched his subjects with jeweled and floral motifs, especially in the small paintings for private clients.

Flaviano Ferramola
(Brescia 1480–1528)

Ferramola's art represents the transition between the late fifteenth-century tradition of Foppa and the innovations made by Romanino in the sixteenth century. Numerous examples of his fresco painting survive in the churches of Santa Maria in Solario and Santa Giulia in Brescia. His work reflects a varied artistic background, and influences from central Italian art.

General Bibliography

Anna Alberti

Archive abbreviations

AMAS, *Archivio dei Musei Civici
d'Arte e Storia di Brescia*
(Brescia Civic Museums Art
and History Archive)

ASB, *Archivio di Stato di Brescia*
(State Archive, Brescia)

ASC, *Archivio Storico Civico, depositato
presso l'Archivio di Stato di Brescia*
(Civic Historic Archive, deposited
at the State Archive, Brescia)

AV, *Archivio Vescovile, Brescia*
(Episcopal Archive, Brescia)

SPASD, AV, *Soprintendenza per il Patrimonio
Storico Artistico e Demoetnoantropologico,
Archivio Vecchio, Milano*
(Historic, Artistic and Demo-ethno-
anthropological Heritage Office, Milan,
Old Archive)

1535

M. Nizzoli, *Marii Nizolii Brixellensis Obseruationum in M.T. Ciceronem prima pars*, Ex Prato Albuini 1535.

1542

S. Speroni, *Dialoghi*, In Vinegia (Venice) 1542.

1547

T. D'Aragona[1], *Dialogo della signora Tullia d'Aragona della infinità di amore*, In Vinegia (Venice) 1547.

T. D'Aragona[2], *Rime della signora Tullia di Aragona, et di diuersi a lei*, In Vinegia (Venice) 1547.

1568

G. Vasari, *Le vite de' piu eccellenti Pittori, Scultori, e architettori scritte Da M. Giorgio Vasari pittore et architetto aretino, Di Nuovo dal Medesimo Riviste Et Ampliate Con i Ritratti loro Et con l'aggiunta delle Vite de' vivi, & de' morti Dall'anno 1550 insino al 1567*, Florence 1568.

1590

C. Vecelio, *De gli habiti antichi, et moderni di diverse parti del mondo libri due, fatti da Cesare Vecellio, & con discorsi da lui dichiarati…*, Venetia (Venice) 1590.

Undated (XVI century)
P. Nassino, *Registro di molte cose seguite*, Brescia, Biblioteca Queriniana, ms. C.I.15.

1630

C. Ripa, *Della più che nouissima Iconologia di Cesare Ripa Perugino Caualier di SS. Mauritio, & Lazaro. Parte prima [-terza]. Nella quale si esprimono varie Imagini di Virtù, Vitij, Affetti, Passioni humane, Arti, Discipline, Humori, Elementi, Corpi celesti, Prouincie d'Italia, Fiumi, & altre materie infinite vtili ad ogni stato di Persone; ampliata dal Sig. cau. Gio. Zaratino Castellini Romano in questa vltima editione di Imagini, & Discorsi, con Indici copiosi, & ricorretta*, In Padoua (Padua) 1630.

Undated (between 1630 and 1669)
B. Faino[1], "Catalogo Delle chiese riuerite in Brescia, et delle pitture et Scolture memorabili, che si uedono in esse in questi tempi", Brescia, Biblioteca Queriniana, ms. E.VII.6 (critic ed. edited by C. Boselli, in *Commentari dell'Ateneo di Brescia per l'anno 1961. Supplemento*).

B. Faino[2], *Pitture Nelle chiese di Brescia*, Brescia, Biblioteca Queriniana, ms. E.I.10 (critic ed. edited by C. Boselli, in *Commentari dell'Ateneo di Brescia per l'anno 1961. Supplemento*).

1642

G. Baglione, *Le Vite de pittori, scultori et architetti. Dal pontificato di Gregorio XIII del 1572 fino a' tempi di Papa Urbano VIII nel 1642*, Rome 1642.

1648

C. Ridolfi, *Le maraviglie dell'arte Overo le vite de gl'illustri pittori veneti, e dello stato*, In Venetia 1648 (German ed. edited by D. von Hadeln, I–II, Berlin 1914–1924; anastatic reprint: Rome 1965).

1660

M. Boschini, *La carta del nauegar pitoresco dialogo tra vn senator venetian deletante, e vn professor de pitura, soto nome d'ecelenza, e de compare. Comparti' in oto venti con i quali la naue venetiana vien conduta in l'alto mar dela pitura, come assoluta dominante de quelo a confusion de chi non intende el bossolo dela calamita*, Venice 1660 (critical ed. edited by A. Pallucchini, Venice – Rome 1966).

1674

M. Boschini, *Le ricche minere della pittura veneziana. Compendiosa informazione di M. B. non solo delle pitture publiche di Venezia, ma dell'isole ancora circonvicine*, Venice 1674.

Undated (between 1675 and 1714)
F. Paglia[1], *Il Giardino Passeggiato della Pittura riflessi di F.P. Dialogo*, [P1]. Brescia, Biblioteca Queriniana, ms. Di Rosa 88.

F. Paglia[2], *Rifflessi. Il giardino della pittura rifflessi di F.P. Compartito in 7 giornate, in cui si scriuono tutte le Opere publiche particolari di Pittura, et di scultura più degne della Città di Brescia Dialogo di F.P. Bresciano*, [P2]. Brescia, Biblioteca Queriniana, ms. G.IV.9 (critical ed. edited by C. Boselli, in *Commentari dell'Ateneo di Brescia per l'anno 1967. Supplemento*).

F. Paglia[3], *Giardino della Pittura di Brescia Diviso in Sette Giornate Opera Di F.P. In Forma di Dialogo Pittura, e Poesia. Libro Primo*, [P3]. Brescia, Biblioteca Queriniana, ms. A.IV.8.

1700

G. A. Averoldo, *Le scelte pitture di Brescia additate al forestiere*, Brescia 1700 (anastatic reprint: Bologna 1977).

1704

P. A. Orlandi, *Abbecedario pittorico nel quale compendiosamente sono descritte le patrie, i maestri, ed i tempi, ne' quali fiorirono circa quattro mila professori di pittura, di scultura, e d'architettura*, Bologna 1704.

1733

G. Baglione, *Le Vite de pittori, scultori, architetti ed intagliatori. Dal pontificato di Gregorio XIII del 1572 fino a' tempi di Papa Urbano VIII nel 1642*, new addition, Naples 1733.

1747

F. Maccarinelli, *Le Glorie di Brescia raccolte dalle Pitture, che nelle sue Chiese, Oratorii, Palazzi, et altri luoghi pubblici sono esposte. Date in luce da me N.N. Sacerdote in Brescia. Nell'anno 1747*, Brescia, Biblioteca Queriniana, ms. I.VIII.29 (critical ed. edited by C. Boselli, in *Commentari dell'Ateneo di Brescia per l'anno 1959. Supplemento*).

1751

F. Maccarinelli, *Le Glorie di Brescia raccolte dalle Pitture Che nelle Chiese di essa, Palazzi, e altri Luoghi pubblici si vedono esposte. Opera data in luce nell'Anno MDCCLI da un Dilettante della Pittura, et arricchita di molte cose, spettanti all'Istoria di Brescia*, Brescia, Biblioteca Queriniana, ms. G.IV.8 (critical ed. edited by C. Boselli, in *Commentari dell'Ateneo di Brescia per l'anno 1959. Supplemento*).

1760

G. B. Carboni, *Le pitture e sculture di Brescia che sono esposte al pubblico con un'appendice di alcune private gallerie*, Brescia 1760 (anastatic reprint: Bologna 1977).

1778

B. Zamboni, *Memorie intorno alle pubbliche fabbriche più insigni della città di Brescia*, Brescia 1778 (anastatic reprint: Bologna 1975).

1789

L. Lanzi, *Storia pittorica della Italia dal Risorgimento delle belle arti fin presso la fine del XVIII secolo*, I–III, Bassano 1789, Tome III.

1795–1796

L. Lanzi, *Storia pittorica della Italia, Tomo II, Parte I, Ove si descrivono alcune scuole della Italia superiore, la Veneziana; e le Lombarde di Mantova, Modena, Parma, Cremona, e Milano*, Bassano 1795–1796.

1807

F. Nicoli Cristiani, *Della Vita e delle Pitture di Lattanzio Gambara. Memorie storiche di Federico Nicoli Cristiani aggiuntevi brevi notizie intorno a' più celebri ed eccellenti pittori bresciani*, Brescia 1807

1809

L. Lanzi, *Storia pittorica della Italia dal Risorgimento delle belle arti fin presso la fine del XVIII secolo. Edizione terza corretta ed accresciuta dall'autore*, I–VI, Bassano 1809, Tome III.

1820

F. Gambara, *Geste de' bresciani durante la Lega di Cambrai. Canti del cavalier Gio. Francesco Gambara*, Brescia 1820.

Galleria di quadri esistenti in casa Fenaroli in Brescia, Brescia 1820.

1823

Atti della I.R. Regia Accademia delle Belle Arti in Milano, 1823.

Esposizione dei grandi e piccoli concorsi ai premi e delle opere degli artisti e dei dilettanti nelle gallerie dell'I.R. Accademia delle Belle Arti per l'anno 1823, Milan 1823.

1826

P. Brognoli, *Nuova guida per la città di Brescia*, Brescia 1826 (anastatic reprint: Brescia 1978).

1834

A. Sala, *Pitture ed altri oggetti di belle arti di Brescia*, Brescia 1834 (anastatic reprint: Brescia 1984).

1837

G. Beretta, *Della vita, delle opere ed opinioni del cav. Giuseppe Longhi*, Milan 1837.

1844

Riepilogo del valore attribuito ai Quadri, Scolture, Cammei, Stampe, Disegni e libri legati alla R.ª Città di Brescia dal fu Signor Conte Paolo Tosio con suo testamento olografo 12 Marzo 1832, ed altre opere d'Arte aggiunte al Sudd.° Legato per generosità dalla Nob. Sig.ra Cont.ª Paolina Bergonzi Tosio, Brescia, Civic Museums Art and History Archive, ms.

1845

C. Ransonnet, *Sopra un dipinto di Alessandro Bonvicino soprannominato il Moretto di Brescia. Discorso del barone Carlo Ransonnet con cenni biografici intorno a questo artista* (Italian version with notes), Brescia 1845.

1846

Oggetti d'arte esistenti nella Galleria Tosio in Brescia, 7 marzo 1846, Brescia, Civic Museums Art and History Archive, ms.

1853

F. Odorici, *Guida di Brescia. Rapporto alle arti e ai monumenti antichi e moderni*, Brescia 1853.

1854

F. Odorici, *La Galleria Tosio ora Pinacoteca Municipale di Brescia*, Brescia 1854.

1861–1867

A. F. Rio, *De l'art chrétien, Nouvelle éd. entièrement refondue et considérablement augmentée*, I–IV, Paris 1861–1867.

1863

F. Odorici, *La Galleria Tosio ora Pinacoteca Municipale di Brescia*, 2nd ed., Brescia 1863.

1868

T. Castellini, *Catalogo dei quadri, scolture, stampe ed altri oggetti d'arte, conservati nella Civica Pinacoteca Tosio compilato nel 1868 dal Pittore Tommaso Castellini custode della Pinacoteca*, Brescia, Civic Museums Art and History Archive, ms.

1871

J. A. Crowe, G. B. Cavalcaselle, *A History of Painting in North Italy, Venice, Padua, Vicenza, Verona, Ferrara, Milan, Friuli, Brescia from the Fourteenth to the Sixteenth Century*, I–II, London 1871.

1875

G. Ariassi, *Catalogo di tutte le opere d'arti belle esistenti nella Pinacoteca Tosio, di proprietà del Municipio di Brescia, Ordinato secondo la collocazione dei lavori d'arte del 1875*, Brescia, Civic Museums Art and History Archive, ms.

1877

S. Fenaroli, *Dizionario degli artisti bresciani*, Brescia 1877 (anastatic reprint: Bologna 1971).

1879

[F. Odorici], *Brescia. La Pinacoteca comunale Tosio*, Brescia 1879 (ed. with author's name: 1883).

1886

G. Biagi, "Un'etéra romana", in *Nuova antologia di scienze, lettere ed arti*, series III, 4, 1886, 16, pp. 655–711.

1888

Brescia. Pinacoteca Comunale Martinengo. Arte antica, Brescia 1888.

[F. Odorici], *La Pinacoteca comunale Tosio*, 2nd ed., Brescia 1888.

1889

G. Frizzoni, "La Pinacoteca comunale Martinengo in Brescia", in *Archivio Storico dell'Arte*, II, 1889, pp. 24–33.

1890

G. Morelli (I. Lermolieff), *Kunstkritische Studien über italienische Malerei. I, Die Galerien Borghese und Doria Panfili in Rom*, Leipzig 1890.

1891

E. Celani, "La vita e le opere di Tullia d'Aragona, cortigiana del secolo XVI", in *Le rime di Tullia d'Aragona, cortigiana del secolo XVI*, edited by E. Celani, Bologna 1891.

1894

Exhibition of Works by the Old Masters, and by Deceased Masters of the British School, exhibition catalog, London 1894.

C. J. Ffoulkes, "Le esposizioni d'arte italiana a Londra", in *Archivio Storico dell'Arte*, VII, 1894, pp. 249–268.

1896

E. Jacobsen, "Die Gemälde der einheimischen Malerschule in Brescia", in *Jahrbuch der königlich preussischen Kunstsammlungen*, XVII, 1896, pp. 19–42.

1898

[P. Da Ponte], *L'opera del Moretto*, Brescia 1898.

L. Frati, "Giuochi ed amori alla corte d'Isabella d'Este", in *Archivio Storico Lombardo*, series III, XXV, 1898, pp. 350–365.

P. Molmenti, *Il Moretto da Brescia*, Florence 1898.

1899

U. Fleres, "La pinacoteca dell'Ateneo in Brescia", in *Le Gallerie Nazionali Italiane*, IV, 1899, pp. 263–291.

1907

B. Berenson, *North Italian Painters of the Renaissance*, New York–London 1907.

1909

The Masterpieces of Moretto da Brescia (c. 1498–c. 1554), London–Glasgow 1909.

1912

J. A. Crowe, G. B. Cavalcaselle, *A History of Painting in North Italy: Venice, Padua, Vicenza, Verona, Ferrara, Milan, Friuli, Brescia from the Fourteenth to the Sixteenth Century*, I–III, T. Borenius (ed.), London 1912.

1917

R. Longhi, "Cose bresciane del Cinquecento", in *L'Arte*, XX, 1917, pp. 99–114 (republished in R. Longhi, *Opere complete*, vol. I, Tome 1, *Scritti giovanili. 1912–1922*, Florence 1956, pp. 327–343).

1925

G. Nicodemi, *Gerolamo Romanino*, Brescia 1925.

S. Ortolani, "Di Gian Girolamo Savoldo", in *L'Arte*, XXVIII, 1925, pp. 163–173.

D. F. von Hadeln, "Notes on Savoldo", in *Art in America and elsewhere*, XIII, 1925, pp. 72–82.

1927

P. Guerrini, "La galleria d'arte del patrizio bresciano Paolo Brognoli. Note e catalogo", in *Commentari dell'Ateneo di Brescia per l'anno 1927*, print 1928, pp. 195–256 (republished in P. Guerrini, *Note d'arte*, Brescia 1985, pp. 127–173).

R. Longhi, "Due dipinti inediti di G.G. Savoldo", in *Vita Artistica*, II, 1927, pp. 72–75 (republished in R. Longhi, *Opere complete*, vol. 2, Tome 1, *Saggi e ricerche* 1925–1928, Florence 1967, pp. 149–155).

[G. Nicodemi], *La Pinacoteca Tosio e Martinengo*, Bologna 1927 (2nd ed., 1931).

1928

A. Venturi[1], "Romanino da Brescia", in *Storia dell'arte italiana*, vol. IX, *La pittura del Cinquecento*, part IV, Milan 1928, pp. 792–856.

A. Venturi[2], *Storia dell'arte italiana,* vol. IX, *La pittura del Cinquecento*, part III, Milan 1928.

1929

R. Longhi, "Quesiti caravaggeschi. II. I precedenti", in *Pinacotheca*, I, 1929, n. 5–6, pp. 258–320 (republished in R. Longhi, *Opere complete*, Vol. IV, "Me pinxit e Quesiti caravaggeschi", Florence 1968, pp. 97–143 and in *Da Cimabue a Morandi. Saggi di storia della pittura italiana scelti e ordinati da Gianfranco Contini*, Milan 1973, pp. 735–800).

A. Venturi, *Storia dell'arte italiana,* vol. IX, *La pittura del Cinquecento*, part IV, Milan 1929.

1931

G. Delogu, *Pittori minori liguri, lombardi, piemontesi del Seicento e del Settecento*, Venice 1931.

1933

G. Lendorff, *Giovanni Battista Moroni. Der Porträitmaler von Bergamo*, Winterthur 1933.

1935

V. Bloch, *I pittori della realtà nel Seicento*, Rome 1935 (taken from *Occidente*, X).

La pittura a Brescia nel Seicento e nel Settecento, exhibition catalog, E. Calabi (ed.), Brescia 1935.

1936

S. Rosati, *Tullia d'Aragona*, Milan 1936.

1938

A. Venturi, *Storia dell'arte italiana,* vol. IX, *La pittura del Cinquecento*, part VII, Milan 1938.

1938–1948

A. M. Hind, *Early italian engraving. A critical catalogue with complete reproduction of all the prints described*, I–VII, London 1938–1948.

1939

La pittura bresciana del Rinascimento, exhibition catalog, F. Lechi, G. Panazza (ed.), Bergamo 1939.

F. Torrefranca, *Il segreto del Quattrocento. Musiche ariose e poesia popolaresca,* Milan 1939.

1940

G. Nicco Fasola, "Lineamenti del Savoldo", in *L'Arte*, XLIII, 1940, pp. 51–81.

1942–1945

C. Boselli, "Appunti al 'Catalogo delle opere d'arte nelle chiese di Brescia' a cura di A. Morassi", in *Commentari dell'Ateneo di Brescia per gli anni 1942(B)–1945*, printed 1947, pp. 75–96.

1943

G. Gombosi, *Moretto da Brescia*, Basel 1943.

1944

R. Pallucchini, *La pittura veneziana del Cinquecento,* I–II, Novara 1944.

1946

[G. Panazza, C. Boselli], *Pitture in Brescia dal Duecento all'Ottocento*, [exhibition catalog], 2nd ed., Brescia 1946.

1948

A. M. Hind, *Early italian engraving. A critical catalogue with complete reproduction of all the prints described*, V.II, *Known masters other than Florentine monogrammists and anonymous*, London 1948.

1949

C. Boselli, "Di secondo e terzo ordine gli scolari del Moretto", in *Giornale di Brescia*, 12 March 1949, p. 3.

1951

La moda in cinque secoli di pittura. 200 opere di maestri d'ogni paese dal 400 all'800, exhibition catalog, Turin 1951.

1953

C. Boselli[1], "Bollettino dei civici musei (1953)", in *Commentari dell'Ateneo di Brescia per l'anno 1953*, printed 1954, pp. 211–214.

C. Boselli[2], "Invito alla Pinacoteca", in *Brescia. Rassegna dell'Ente provinciale per il turismo*, IV, 14, 1953, pp. 18–23.

C. Boselli[3], "Luca Mombello pittore", in *Terra nostra*, 1953, 7, pp. 13–14.

I pittori della realtà in Lombardia, exhibition catalog, R. Cipriani, G. Testori (ed.), Milan 1953.

F. C. Legrand, F. Sluys, 'Têtes composées du XV Siècle à nos jours", in *Beaux Arts*, 17, 617, 1953.

R. Longhi, "Dal Moroni al Ceruti", in *I pittori della realtà in Lombardia*, exhibition catalog edited by R. Cipriani and G. Testori, Milan 1953, pp. I–XIX.

1954

C. Boselli, "Il Moretto, 1498–1554", in *Commentari dell'Ateneo di Brescia per l'anno 1954. Supplemento*.

B. Geiger, *I dipinti ghiribizzosi di Giuseppe Arcimboldi, pittore illusionista del Cinquecento (1527–1593)*, Florence 1954.

F. C. Legrand, F. Sluys, "Some Little-known 'Arcimboldeschi'", in *The Burlington Magazine*, XVCI, 616, 1954, pp. 210–214.

1955

"Arcimboldi", in *Selearte*, n. 21, 1955, p. 31.

1956

J. Bousquet, "Der Mensch als Sammelsurium aus der Porträtgalerie der kaiserlichen 'Hofconterfeter' Giuseppe Arcimboldo", in *Die Kunst und das Schöne Heim*, 1956.

1958
C. Boselli, "[Recensione a] Gaetano Panazza, I civici musei e la Pinacoteca di Brescia, Bergamo 1958", in *Archivio Storico Lombardo*, series VIII, 8, 1958, pp. 333–336.

G. Panazza, *I Civici Musei e la Pinacoteca di Brescia*, Bergamo 1958.

1959
C. Boselli, "Francesco Maccarinelli, Le glorie di Brescia 1747–1751 (Biblioteca Queriniana Ms. I.VIII.29 e G.IV.8)", in *Commentari dell'Ateneo di Brescia per l'anno 1959. Supplemento*.

C. E. Gilbert, "Portraits by and near Romanino", in *Arte Lombarda*, IV, 1959, 2, pp. 261–267.

G. Panazza, *Pinacoteca civica Tosio Martinengo, Brescia. Con l'elenco delle opere*, Milan 1959 (2nd ed., 1964).

1961
C. Boselli, "Bernardino Faino. Catalogo delle Chiese di Brescia (Manoscritti Queriniani E.VII.6 ed E.I.10)", in *Commentari dell'Ateneo di Brescia per l'anno 1961. Supplemento*.

M. L. Ferrari, *Il Romanino*, Milan 1961.

M. Roethlisberger, *Claude Lorrain. The Paintings*, New-Haven 1961.

1962
L'ideale classico del Seicento in Italia e la pittura di paesaggio, exhibition catalog, Bologna 1962.

1963
A. Boschetto, *Giovan Gerolamo Savoldo*, Milan 1963.

R. Bossaglia, "La pittura del Cinquecento. I maggiori e i loro scolari", in *Storia di Brescia*, II, Brescia 1963, pp. 1011–1101.

G. Gamulin, "Qualche aggiunta alla pittura lombarda", in *Arte Lombarda*, VIII.2, 1963, pp. 260–265.

G. Panazza, "La pittura nella seconda metà del Quattrocento", in *Storia di Brescia*, II, Brescia 1963, pp. 949–1010

L. Salerno, *Salvator Rosa*, Milan 1963.

1963–1964
Storia di Brescia, edited by G. Treccani degli Alfieri, I–V, Brescia 1963–1964.

1964
P. V. Begni Redona, "La pittura manieristica", in *Storia di Brescia*, III, Brescia 1964, pp. 527–588.

G. Panazza, "Le arti applicate connesse alla pittura del Rinascimento", in *Storia di Brescia*, III, Brescia 1964, pp. 677–700.

B. Passamani, "La pittura dei secoli XVII–XVIII", in *Storia di Brescia*, III, Brescia 1964, pp. 589–676.

1965
F. Kossoff, "Romanino in Brescia", in *The Burlington Magazine*, CVII, 715, 1965, pp. 514–521.

G. Panazza, in association with A. Damiani and B. Passamani, *Mostra di Girolamo Romanino*, exhibition catalog, 2nd ed., Brescia 1965.

L. Procacci, U. Procacci, "Il carteggio di Marco Boschini con il cardinale Leopoldo de' Medici", in *Saggi & memorie di storie dell'arte*, IV, 1965, pp. 85–113.

1966
A. Ballarin, *Gerolamo Savoldo*, Milan 1966.

O. Marini, "Qualcosa per la vicenda del 'Pitocchetto'. I, I committenti bresciani del Ceruti; A) il Ceruti nella Galleria Barbisoni", in *Paragone*, 199, 1966, pp. 34–42.

G. Testori, "Giacomo Ceruti (lingua e dialetto nella tradizione bresciana)", in *Giacomo Ceruti. Mostra di 32 opere inedite*, Milan 1966, pp. III–XXXI (republished in *Invito al Ceruti. Pittore in lingua bresciana*, Brescia 1987, pp. 42–71, and in *La realtà della pittura. Scritti di storia e critica d'arte dal Quattrocento al Settecento*, P. Marani [ed.], Milan 1995, pp. 429–456).

1967
C. Boselli, "Francesco Paglia. Il giardino della pittura (Manoscritti Queriniani G.IV.9 e Di Rosa 8)", in *Commentari dell'Ateneo di Brescia per l'anno 1967. Supplemento*.

A. Morassi, "Giacomo Ceruti detto il 'Pitocchetto' pittore verista", in *Pantheon*, XXV, 1967, pp. 348–367.

1968
F. Lechi, *I quadri della collezione Lechi in Brescia. Storia e documenti*, Florence 1968.

O. Marini, "Qualcosa per la vicenda del 'Pitocchetto'. I, I committenti bresciani del Ceruti: il Ceruti nella Galleria Avogadro", in *Paragone*, 215, 1968, pp. 40–58.

G. Panazza, *La Pinacoteca e i Musei di Brescia*, new revised and expanded edition, Bergamo 1968.

1970
M. Roethlisberger-Bianco, *Cavalier Pietro Tempesta and his Time*, Newark 1970.

1971
C. Boselli, "Nuove fonti per la storia dell'arte. L'archivio dei conti Gambara presso la Civica Biblioteca Queriniana di Brescia. I. Il carteggio", in *Memorie, Istituto veneto di scienze, lettere ed arti. Classe di scienze morali lettere ed arti*, 35, 1971, 1.

G. C. Sciolla, *L'arte dei Piazza*, in A.

Novasconi, *I Piazza*, Lodi 1971, pp. 11–30.

1972
B. B. Fredericksen, F. Zeri, *Census of Pre-Nineteenth Century Italian Paintings in North American Public Collections*, Cambridge (Mass.) 1972.

1973
C. M. Kauffmann, *Victoria and Albert Museum. Catalogue of foreign paintings*, I–II, London 1973.

1974
F. Lechi[1], *Le dimore bresciane in cinque secoli di storia*, II, *Il Quattrocento*, Brescia 1974.

F. Lechi[2], *Le dimore bresciane in cinque secoli di storia*, V, *Il Seicento*, Brescia 1974.

G. Panazza, C. Boselli, *La Pinacoteca Tosio Martinengo*, Milan 1974.

1977
C. Boselli, *Regesto artistico dei notai roganti in Brescia dall'anno 1500 all'anno 1560*, I–II, Brescia 1977.

1977–1980
L. Salerno, *Pittori di paesaggio del Seicento a Roma*, I–III, Rome 1977–1980.

1978
L. Anelli, *Grazio Cossali. Pittore orceano*, Orzinuovi 1978.

P. V. Begni Redona, G. Vezzoli, *Lattanzio Gambara pittore*, Brescia 1978.

[G. Ferri Pittaluga], "Biografie. 12, Andrea Fantoni", in *I Fantoni. Quattro secoli di bottega di scultura in Europa*, R. Bossaglia (ed.), Vicenza 1978, pp. 79–83.

1979
Giovan Battista Moroni (1520–1578), exhibition catalog, M. Gregori (ed.), Bergamo 1979.

M. Gregori[1], "Giovan Battista Moroni. Tutte le opere", in *I pittori bergamaschi dal XIII al XIX secolo. Il Cinquecento*, III, Bergamo 1979, pp. 97–377.

M. Gregori[2], "Introduzione al Moroni", in *Giovan Battista Moroni (1520–1578)*, exhibition catalog, M. Gregori (ed.), Bergamo 1979, pp. 17–68.

F. Luisi, *Apografo miscellaneo marciano. Frottole, canzoni e madrigali con alcuni alla pavana in villanesco*, Venice 1979.

F. Porzio, *L'universo illusorio di Arcimboldi*, Milan 1979 (new ed., 1987).

R. Stradiotti, "Maestro bresciano, fine sec. XV", entry in *Brescia romana. Materiali per un museo. II*, II, pp. 149–154.

1980
E. Lucchesi Ragni, "Alessandro Moretto, Annunciazione", entry in *Bergamo per Lorenzo Lotto. Lorenzo Lotto, riflessioni lombarde*, Congress proceedings (Bergamo 1980); *Omaggio a Lorenzo Lotto*, exhibition catalog (Bergamo 1980–1981), Bergamo 1980, pp. 95–98.

F. Rossi, "Giovanni Battista Moroni, Il profeta Mosè", entry in *Bergamo per Lorenzo Lotto*, Bergamo 1980, pp. 129–131.

1981
L. Anelli, "Una ignota 'Maddalena' di Luca Mombello", in *Commentari dell'Ateneo di Brescia per l'anno 1981*, print 1982, pp. 289–293.

V. Guazzoni, *Moretto. Il tema sacro*, Brescia 1981.

R. Stradiotti, "Francesco Paglia", in *Società e cultura nella Brescia del Settecento*. III, *Brescia pittorica 1700–1760. L'immagine del sacro*, exhibition catalog, Brescia 1981, pp. 27–31.

1982
P. Dal Poggetto, "Antonio Cifrondi", in *I pittori bergamaschi dal XIII al XIX secolo. Il Settecento*, I, Bergamo 1982, pp. 357–619.

M. Gregori, *Giacomo Ceruti*, Cinisello Balsamo (Milan) 1982.

1983
E. M. Guzzo, "Francesco Paglia in S. Maria in Organo a Verona e il misterioso Francesco Bernardi detto il Bagolaro", in *Brixia Sacra*, new series, XVIII, 1983, pp. 123–124.

1984
The Illustrated Bartsch, 37. Formerly vol. 17 (part 4). Italian Masters of the Sixteenth Century. Antonio Tempesta, S. Buffa (ed.), New York 1984.

1985
G. Agosti, "Giovanni Morelli corrispondente di Niccolò Antinori", in *Studi e ricerche di collezionismo e museografia. Florence 1820–1920*, Pisa 1985, pp. 1–83.

L. Anelli, "Un Paglia inedito", in *Il Giornale di Brescia*, 6 September 1985.

K. C[hristiansen], "Giovanni Gerolamo Savoldo", in *The Age of Caravaggio*, exhibition catalog, New York–Milan, 1985, pp. 79–85.

C. Gilbert, "Lo stile nelle firme del Savoldo", in *Giovanni Gerolamo Savoldo pittore bresciano. Atti del convegno (Brescia, 21–22 maggio 1983)*, G. Panazza (ed.), Brescia 1985, pp. 21–28.

M. Mondini, "I dipinti della collezione Avogadro in Rezzato da un inventario settecentesco", in *Rezzato. Materiali per una storia*, P. Corsini, G.B. Tirelli (ed.), Rezzato 1985, pp. 117–122.

M. T. Rosa Barezzani, "Musica e strumenti musicali nelle opere del Savoldo", in *Giovanni Gerolamo Savoldo pittore bresciano. Atti del convegno (Brescia, 21–22 maggio 1983)*, G. Panazza (ed.), Brescia 1985, pp. 113–128.

C. Slim, "Giovanni Girolamo Savoldo's Portrait of a Man with a Recorder", in *Early Music*, XIII, 1985, 3, pp. 398–406.

The Travel Diaries of Otto Mündler 1855–1858, edited and indexed by C. Togneri Dowd, in production by J. Anderson. [Edited by Walpole Society, 51, 1985].

1986
P. V. Begni Redona, "Lattanzio Gambara", entry in *Pittura del Cinquecento a Brescia*, Milan 1986, pp. 245–247.

F. Frangi, [Entries], in *Pittura del Cinquecento a Brescia*, Milan 1986, pp. 167–201.

S. Guerrini, "Note e documenti per la storia dell'arte bresciana dal XVI al XVIII secolo", in *Brixia Sacra*, new series, XXI, 1986, pp. 3–84.

A. Lugli, "Arte e meraviglia, antico, Novecento, contemporaneo", in *XLII Esposizione internazionale d'arte La Biennale di Venezia. Arte e scienza. Catalogo generale, 1986*, Venice 1986, pp. 119–120.

M. Mondini, C. Zani, "La decorazione di palazzo Calini in Brescia tra rococò e neoclassico", in *Dai Civici musei d'arte e di storia di Brescia. Studi e notizie*, 2, 1986, printed 1988, pp. 47–76.

R. Prestini, *La chiesa di Sant'Alessandro in Brescia. Storia ed arte*, Brescia 1986.

Pittura del Cinquecento a Brescia, Milan 1986.

1987
K. Christiansen, "Dates and Non-dates in Savoldo's Paintings", in *The Burlington Magazine*, CXXIX, 1007, 1987, pp. 80–81.

B. Passamani, *Brescia e Ceruti. Patrizi, popolo, pitocchi. Alla ricerca di 'fatti certi' e di 'persone vere'*, in *Giacomo Ceruti. Il Pitocchetto*, exhibition catalog, Milan 1987, pp. 11–28.

R. Stradiotti, "Francesco Paglia, Natività del Battista", entry in *I pittori bergamaschi dal XIII al XIX secolo. Il Seicento*, IV, Bergamo 1987, p. 248.

U. Vaglia, *I Calini, nobile famiglia bresciana*, Brescia 1987.

1988
Alessandro Bonvicino, il Moretto, exhibition catalog, Bologna 1988.

L. Anelli[1], "Di due Moretto e di alcune cose morettesche", in *Notizie da Palazzo Albani*, XVI, 1998, 2, pp. 55–69.

L. Anelli[2], "Venetismo di un gruppo di dipinti bresciani del Cinquecento. Mombello, Galeazzi, Gandino, Cossali", in *Arte Veneta*, XLII, 1988 (print 1989), pp. 77–86.

P. V. Begni Redona, *Alessandro Bonvicino. Il Moretto da Brescia*, Brescia 1988.

F. Frangi, "Floriano, Ferramola (Brescia, 1480 circa–1527/1528)", in *La Pittura in Italia. Il Cinquecento*, new revised and expanded edition, I–II, Milan 1988, pp. 711–712.

E. M. Guzzo, "Arte in Valtrompia", in *Brixia Sacra*, new series, XXII, 1988, pp. 27–44.

B. Passamani, *Guida della Pinacoteca Tosio Martinengo di Brescia*, Brescia 1988.

R. Stradiotti, "Moretto. Prime indagini conoscitive", in *Alessandro Bonvicino, il Moretto*, exhibition catalog, Bologna 1988, pp. 203–222.

La pittura del '500 in Valtrompia, exhibition catalog, C. Sabatti (ed.), Brescia 1988 (2nd revised ed. 2000).

Suppellettile ecclesiastica, I, B. Montevecchi, S. Vasco Rocca (ed.), (Terminological Dictionaries, 4), Florence 1988 (printed 1987).

1989
E. Battisti, *L'antirinascimento*, I–II, Milan 1989.

A. Morandotti, "Antonio Rasio", entry in *La natura morta in Italia*, F. Porzio (ed.), Milan 1989, p. 280.

A. Morandotti, M. Natale, "La natura morta in Lombardia", in *La natura morta in Italia*, F. Porzio (ed.), Milan 1989, pp. 196–215.

R. Prestini, "La chiesa e il convento in cinque secoli di storia", in V. Volta, R. Prestini, P. V. Begni Redona, *La chiesa e il convento di San Giuseppe in Brescia*, Brescia 1989, pp. 61–176.

R. Stradiotti, "Gerolamo Romanino e aiuti (Callisto Piazza?), La Pietà tra i Santi Paolo, Giuseppe e le Mitrie", entry in *I Piazza da Lodi. Una tradizione di pittori nel Cinquecento*, edited by G.C. Sciolla, Milan 1989, pp. 194–195.

V. Volta, "Le vicende edilizie del convento dei Minori Osservanti di San Giuseppe in Brescia", in V. Volta, R. Prestini, P. V. Begni Redona, *La chiesa e il convento di San Giuseppe in Brescia*, Brescia 1989, pp. 9–60.

1990
A. Ballarin, "Profilo del Savoldo", congress report in *Savoldo e la cultura figurativa del suo tempo tra Veneto e Lombardia* (Brescia, 1990).

A. Gentili, "Savoldo, il ritratto e l'allegoria musicale", in *Giovanni Gerolamo, Savoldo: tra Foppa, Giorgione e Caravaggio*, exhibition catalog, Milan 1990, pp. 65–70.

M. Olivari, "Una sconosciuta Immacolata di Francesco Paglia", in *Brera. Notizie dalla Pinacoteca*, 19, 1990, p. 4.

1991
J. K. Cadogan, "Unknown North Italian, 17th Century, Spring, Summer", entry in

Wadsworth Atheneum Paintings. II. Italy and Spain. Fourteenth Through Nineteenth Centuries, J.K. Cadogan (ed.), Hartford 1991, pp. 268–270.

C. Michel, *Le voyage d'Italie de Charles-Nicolas Cochin (1758),* Edité en facsimile avec une introduction et des notes, Rome 1991.

1991–1993
E. Lucchesi Ragni, "Floriano Ferramola e la 'bellissima' sala di palazzo Calini", in *Museo Bresciano. Studi e notizie dai Musei Civici d'arte e storia,* 5, 1991– 1993 (published in 1995), pp. 23–43.

1992
G. Agosti, C. Zani, "Sul Moretto in casa Ugoni", in *Il ritorno dei Profeti. Un ciclo di affreschi del Moretto per Brescia,* exhibition catalog, Brescia 1992, pp. 17–37.

L. Anelli, "Moretteschi bresciani del secondo Cinquecento e del Seicento. Da Luca Mombello a Tommaso Bona", in *Civiltà bresciana,* I, 1992, 1, pp. 23–47.

F. Gonzáles Bernáldez, "Caratteristiche basilari della natura mediterranea", in *Paesaggio mediterraneo,* exhibition catalog, Seville 1992, pp. 42–45, 47.

La cornice italiana. Dal Rinascimento al Neoclassico, edited by F. Sabatelli, Milan 1992.

1993
A. Ballarin, "Girolamo di Romano, dit Romanino", entry in *Le siècle de Titien. L'âge d'or de la peinture à Venice,* exhibition catalog, M. Laclotte (ed.), 2nd ed., Paris 1993, pp. 443–449.

1993–1995
V. Frati, I. Gianfranceschi, F. Robecchi, *La Loggia di Brescia e la sua piazza. Evoluzione di un fulcro urbano nella storia di mezzo millennio,* I–III, Brescia 1993–1995.

1994
A. Nova, *Girolamo Romanino,* Turin 1994.

P. Ovidio Nasone, *Metamorfosi,* edited by P. Bernardini Marzolla, Turin 1994.

M. S. Proni, *Giacomo Francesco Cipper detto il 'Todeschini',* Soncino 1994.

R. Stradiotti, [Entries], in *La pittura del '600 in Valtrompia. Restauri e proposte di restauro,* exhibition catalog, C. Sabatti (ed.), Gardone Val Trompia–Villa Carcina 1994.

1995
I. Lechi, "La collezione Avogadro di Brescia", in *Arte Lombarda,* 113–115, 1995, pp. 170–180.

R. Longhi, "I preparatori del Naturalismo. 1910–1911", in *Il palazzo non finito. Saggi inediti 1910–1926,* F. Frangi, C. Montagnani (ed.), Milan 1995, pp. 11–32.

E. Lucchesi Ragni, "Gli affreschi di Floriano Ferramola nel salone di palazzo Calini", in V. Frati, I. Gianfranceschi, F. Robecchi, *La Loggia di Brescia e la sua piazza. Evoluzione di un fulcro urbano nella storia di mezzo millennio,* II, *La costruzione del palazzo (1492–1574),* Brescia 1995, pp. 107–111.

1996
L. Anelli, *Pietro Bellotti, 1625–1700,* Brescia 1996.

Annicco, edited by V. Guazzoni, Casalmorano 1996.

S. Bizzotto Passamani, "Floriano Ferramola", *ad vocem,* in *Dizionario biografico degli italiani,* vol. XLVI, Rome 1996, pp. 435–437.

Immagini del sentire. I cinque sensi nell'arte, exhibition catalog, S. Ferino– Pagden (ed.), Milan 1996.

A. Morandotti, "Le stampe di traduzione come fonti per la storia del collezionismo. Il caso di Milano fra età napoleonica e restaurazione", in *Il Lombardo-Veneto. 1814–1859. Storia e cultura,* N. Dacrema (ed.), Pasian di Prato 1996, pp. 193–237.

1997
M. Capella, "Tra rinnovamento e tradizione. Note per la ridefinizione della vicenda artistica e biografica di Floriano Ferramola", in *Artes,* 5, 1997, pp. 85–110.

I. Gianfranceschi, E. Lucchesi Ragni, "Alessandro Bonvicino, gen. Moretto da Brescia, Tullia von Aragon", in *Vittoria Colonna. Dichterin und Muse Michelangelos,* exhibition catalog, S. Ferino–Pagden (ed.), Vienna–Milan, 1997, pp. 209–212.

C. Rigoni, "Fiamminghi a Vicenza", in *La pittura fiamminga nel Veneto e nell'Emilia,* C. Limentani Virdis (ed.), Verona 1997, pp. 133–165.

1998
S. Buganza, "Floriano Ferramola rivisitato", in *Arte Cristiana,* LXXXVI, 1998, pp. 121–138.

F. Frangi, "L'immagine dei poveri tra genere, realtà e cultura assistenziale. Riflessioni in margine al ciclo di Padernello di Giacomo Ceruti", in *Da Caravaggio a Ceruti. La scena di genere e l'immagine dei pitocchi nella pittura italiana,* exhibition catalog, F. Porzio (ed.), Milan 1998, pp. 43–61.

G. Gruber, [Entries], in *Da Caravaggio a Ceruti. La scena di genere e l'immagine dei pitocchi nella pittura italiana,* exhibition catalog, F. Porzio (ed.), Milano 1998.

M. C. Terzaghi[1], "Giacomo Ceruti, detto il Pitocchetto, I due pitocchi", entry in *L'anima e il volto. Ritratto e fisiognomica da Leonardo a Bacon,* exhibition catalog, F. Caroli (ed.), Milan 1998, p. 350.

M. C. Terzaghi[2], [Entries], in *Da Caravaggio a Ceruti. La scena di genere e l'immagine dei pitocchi nella pittura italiana*, exhibition catalog, F. Porzio (ed.), Milan 1998.

C. Zani, "Giacomo Ceruti, Il ciclo di Padernello", entry in *Da Caravaggio a Ceruti. La scena di genere e l'immagine dei pitocchi nella pittura italiana,* exhibition catalog, F. Porzio (ed.), Milan 1998, pp. 431–432.

1999
Giuseppe Longhi, 1766–1831 e la scuola d'incisione dell'Accademia di Brera, A. Crespi (ed.), Monza 1999.

C. Parisio, *La pittura bresciana dei secoli XV e XVI negli scritti inediti di Giovanni Battista Cavalcaselle*, Brescia 1999.

2000
E. Fahy, *L'archivio storico fotografico di Stefano Bardini. Dipinti, disegni, miniature, stampe*, Florence 2000.

P. Humfrey[1], "Canon Bartolomeo Borghi", entry in *Giovanni Battista Moroni. Renaissance Portaitist,* exhibition catalog, Kimbell Art Museum, P. Humfrey (ed.), Fort Worth 2000, p. 69.

P. Humfrey[2], "'Il loro vero e naturale ritratto'. Moroni as Portrait Painter", in *Giovanni Battista Moroni. Renaissance Portaitist,* exhibition catalog, Kimbell Art Museum, P. Humfrey (ed.), Fort Worth 2000, pp. 27–35.

2001
J. Burckhardt, *La pittura italiana del Rinascimento,* M. Ghelardi, S. Müller (ed.), Venice 2001.

M. Capella, "I cicli pittorici di Floriano Ferramola", in *San Salvatore-Santa Giulia a Brescia. Il monastero nella storia*, R. Stradiotti (ed.), Brescia–Milan 2001, pp. 201–209.

D. Princivalli, "Francesco Santacroce", in *Musica e Storia*, IX, 2001, 2, pp. 307–374.

2001–2002
G. Jansen, B. W. Meijer, P. Squellati Brizio, *Repertory of Dutch and Flemish Paintings in Italian Public Collections. II. Lombardy, I–II,* Milan 2001–2002.

2002
Michael Sweerts (1618–1664), exhibition catalog, G. Jansen, P. C. Sutton (ed.), Zwolle 2002.

2003
G. Agosti, "Vincenzo Foppa, da vecchio", in *Vincenzo Foppa*, edited by G. Agosti, M. Natale and G. Romano, Milan–Brescia 2003, pp. 51–69.

2004
A. Bayer, *Painters of Reality: The Legacy of Leonardo and Caravaggio in Lombardy*, exhibition catalog, Metropolitan Museum of Art, New York, 2004

A. Litta, "Modelli di Moroni", in *Giovan Battista Moroni. Lo sguardo sulla realtà, 1560–1579*, exhibition catalog, S. Facchinetti (ed.), Cinisello Balsamo (Milan) 2004, pp. 111–129.

N. Penny, *The Sixteenth Century Italian Paintings*, I, *Paintings from Bergamo, Brescia and Cremona, (National Gallery catalogues)*, London 2004.

M. Valotti, "Il patrimonio artistico", in G. Bocchio, M. Valotti, *La chiesa di S. Quirico a Muscoline. Appunti di storia e arte*, Muscoline 2004, pp. 34–51.

2006
I. Gianfranceschi, E. Lucchesi Ragni, "Alessandro Bonvicino detto il Moretto, Cristo cade sotto il peso della croce", entry in *Da Romanino e Moretto a Ceruti. Tesori ritrovati della Pinacoteca Tosio Martinengo*, exhibition catalog edited by E. Lucchesi Ragni, R. Stradiotti, Conegliano 2006, pp. 82–89.

Photo Credits

© Archivio Fotografico Comune di Brescia - Assessorato al Turismo: 14
© Mauro Pini: 19
© Archivio fotografico Civici Musei d'Arte e Storia - Foto Rapuzzi: 16–19, 30, 32–36, 51, 55, 57, 58–59, 63, 66–67, 69, 73, 74, 77, 81, 83, 87, 91, 95, 98–99, 105–106, 109, 111, 114–115, 118–119, 123–125, 127, 129–130, 132–135, 136, 139–140, 143, 145, 149
© Musée d'Art et d'Histoire, Cognac: 101
© Panajotov collection, Zagabria: 117
© Wadsworth Atheneum Museum of Art, Hartford, Connecticut: 126, 130
© 2006 Fine Arts Museum of San Francisco: 129
© River Collection, Paris: 129

Printed for Linea d'ombra Libri
by Grafiche Antiga, Cornuda (Treviso)
Italy
April 2006